Introduction

This book supports children preparing for the 11+ entrance exam. The
the book are carefully modelled after past papers to ensure that the papers as a whole provide a rich and varied practice to meet all requirements of 11+ maths with an appropriate difficulty.

Papers are designed to teach students the most easily applicable, reusable and fastest solutions to typical problems, and utilise problems which target areas of maths that children typically forget under the pressure of an exam. Solutions provided have been reviewed by many children to ensure that they are easily understandable while being the fastest and most re-applicable.

Each practice paper becomes progressively more complex as you work through the paper. They require the basic knowledge of arithmetical operations of addition, subtraction, multiplication and division, simple algebra, up to level 5 of the National Curriculum (Key Stage 2). Most questions involve straightforward mathematical calculations. Some questions are designed to test a child's ability to extract the necessary information to solve a mathematical problem from questions worded in English. The paper is designed not only for children to prepare for admission exams but also for those aiming for scholarship.

After completing these practice papers, you should be able to:
1. Quickly formulate optimal solutions to any 11+ maths question.
2. More readily apply previously learnt skills on a question to question basis.

11+ Maths Practice Papers comprises of 2 books. Each book contains 4 full practice papers, while each practice paper contains 30 questions and solutions.

Contents

1	Paper 5	1
2	Paper 6	17
3	Paper 7	32
4	Paper 8	45
5	Paper 5 solutions	57
6	Paper 6 solutions	72
7	Paper 7 solutions	85
8	Paper 8 solutions	97

Paper 5

Materials
For this paper you must have:
- Pen, pencil, eraser and ruler.

Time allowed
1 hour.

Instructions
- Aim to complete as much as you can in the time given, without making mistakes.
- You must answer the questions in the space provided.
- Show all your working. You may be awarded marks for correct working even if your final answer is incorrect, and a correct answer unsupported by correct working may not receive full marks.
- Diagrams are not accurately drawn, unless otherwise indicated.
- Calculators are **NOT** allowed.

Information
- There are 30 questions on this paper
- The marks for questions are shown in brackets.
- The maximum mark is 100.

Advice
- Read each question carefully before you start to answer it.
- Keep an eye on the time.
- Don't worry if you don't complete the paper. If you get stuck, just go on to the next question and if you have time at the end come back to the one(s) you left.

1   Work out the following:

1(a) $32 - 6 \times 3 + 12$

Answer……………………………   (1 mark)

1(b) $9^2 - 8^2$

Answer……………………………   (1 mark)

1(c) $11^2 - 9^2$

Answer……………………………   (1 mark)

1(d) $4 \div 0.02$

Answer……………………………   (1 mark)

2   What number is:

2(a)   Six less than -10

Answer……………………………   (1 mark)

2(b)   Twelve more than −8

              Answer…………………………   (1 mark)

3(a)   What is 30% of 40?

              Answer…………………………   (1 mark)

3(b)   What is $\frac{2}{3}$ of 81

              Answer…………………………   (1 mark)

4   Calculate how much bigger $3\frac{1}{2}$ is than $1\frac{3}{4}$

       Give your answer as a decimal.

              Answer…………………………   (2 marks)

5   The sums below were correct before someone rubbed out the brackets. Write down the correct sums, including the brackets.

5(a) $9 - 6 + 4 = -1$ (1 mark)

5(b) $11 - 12 + 3 - 4 = 0$ (1 mark)

....

....

6   The distance from Calais to Paris is 200 miles.

       5 miles is approximately 8 kilometres.

       Calculate the approximate distance in kilometres from Calais to Paris.

       ....

       ....

       ....

              Answer................................   (2 marks)

7   Here are the numbers of music CDs which the 6 students had.

Name	Jack	Emma	Lucy	Mark	Kath	Sam
Number	5	7	15	19	15	11

7(a)   What is the mode?

       ....

       ....

       ....

              Answer................................   (2 marks)

7(b)   What is the median?

       ....

       ....

              Answer................................   (2 marks)

7(c)   What is the range?

       ....

       ....

              Answer................................   (2 marks)

7(d)   What is the mean?

....
....
....

    Answer................................   (2 marks)

8   Write down the next two terms in each of the following sequences:

8(a)   6, 12, 18, 24, ..., ...

....
....
....

    Answer................................   (2 marks)

8(b)   60, 52, 44, 36, ..., ...

....
....
....

    Answer................................   (2 marks)

8(c)   2, 4, 8, 16, ..., ...

....
....
....

    Answer................................   (2 marks)

8(d)   10, 22, 32, 40, ..., ...

....
....
....

    Answer................................   (2 marks)

9   Place the following numbers in descending order:

   $\frac{4}{5}$ 0.6 $\frac{3}{4}$ 0.7 $\frac{2}{3}$

   Answer.................................   (2 marks)

10   Write down two numbers that add to 15 and multiply to 54.

   Answer.................................   (2 marks)

11   A box holds 6 cakes. How many boxes are needed to store 75 cakes?

   Answer.................................   (2 marks)

12   Which volume can give the best estimate of the capacity of a tea cup?
   Circle your answer.

   0.25 litres   0.5 litres   0.75 litres   1 litre   1.25 litres

   Answer.................................   (2 marks)

13 You are given the number 3975. You are allowed to swap the position of any two digits.

13(a) What is the largest possible number you can make using one swap?

....
....
....

Answer................................ (2 marks)

13(b) What is the smallest possible number you can make using one swap?

....
....
....

Answer................................ (2 marks)

14 Jack is 2 years and 8 months older than his sister Emma. Jack is 12 years and 6 months old.

How old is Emma?

....
....
....

Answer................................ (2 marks)

15 Children are offered a 25% discount on the cost of an adult ticket to see a film. Senior citizens are given a 20% discount.

If a child's ticket costs £30, how much does a senior citizen pay?

....
....
....
....
....

Answer................................ (2 marks)

16 The figure shows two identical overlapping triangles. Three sevenths of each triangle is shaded.

What fraction of the whole figure is shaded?

....
....
....
....
....

Answer.............................. (2 marks)

17 Jack and Emma start at the same point on the toy room floor and walk in opposite direction for 100 cm. Each then turns left and walks 80 cm. Finally each of them turns left again and walks 100 cm. How far apart are they then?

....
....
....
....
....
....
....
....
....

Answer.............................. (2 marks)

18 The pie chart shows data collected in a survey by a PE teacher about the favourite sports of a group of 96 school children. $\frac{1}{3}$ of the children preferred football.

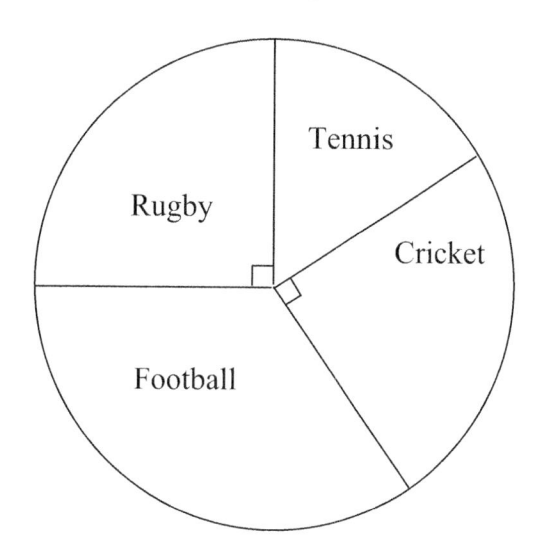

18(a) Work out the angle of the football sector.

....
....
....

Answer............................... (2 marks)

18(b) Write down the fraction of the school children who liked tennis.
Give your answer in the simplest form.

....
....
....
....

Answer............................... (2 marks)

18(c) How many children preferred Rugby?

....
....
....

Answer............................... (2 marks)

20 This graph represents the journeys of a cyclist and a motorist. The motorist is faster than the cyclist.

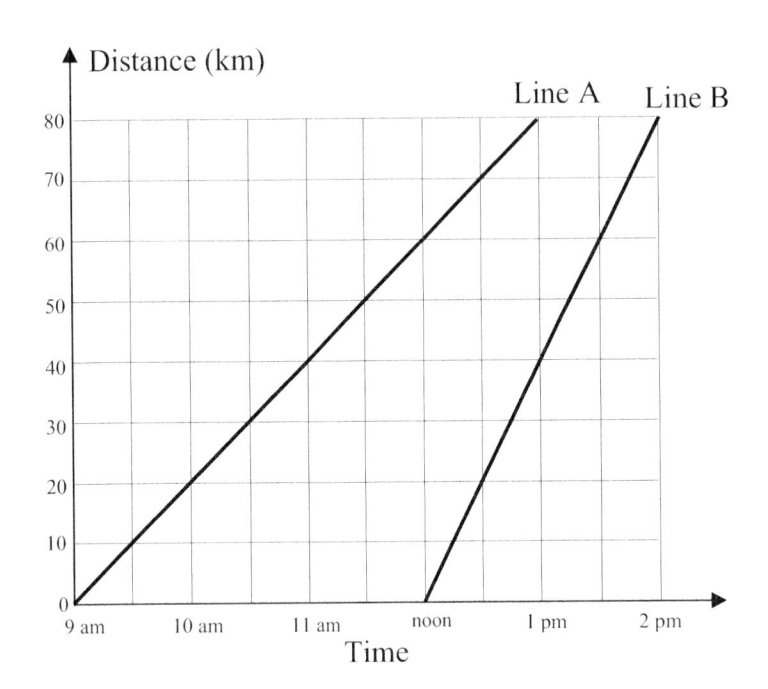

20(a) Which line represents the journey of the motorist?

....

....

....

....

Answer................................ (2 marks)

20(b) At what speed was the cyclist travelling?

....

....

....

Answer................................ (2 marks)

20(c) At what speed was the motorist travelling?

....

....

....

Answer................................ (2 marks)

21 There are thirty pupils in a class. Ten pupils wear glasses. Sixteen pupils are girls. Of the sixteen girls, two wear glasses.

Enter this information into the table below. Then complete the rest of the table.

	Wear glasses	Not wear glasses	Total
Boys			
Girls			
Total			

(3 marks)

....
....

22 There are three numbers. One is a multiple of 14; and the other two are different factors of 55. The sum of the three numbers is greater than fifty but less than sixty. Work out the three numbers.

....
....
....
....
....

Answer…………………………… (3 marks)

23 This is a magic square.

All the columns, rows and diagonals add up to 15.

Several numbers have been missed out.

Fill the remaining squares with numbers obeying this rule.

		6
	5	1

(3 marks)

24 The notation 4! is used as an abbreviation for the product $4\times3\times2\times1$ so that $4!=24$.

Similarly, $9!=9\times8\times7\times6\times5\times4\times3\times2\times1=362880$.

Work out the value of

24(a) 5!

Answer................................ (2 marks)

24(b) 10!

Answer................................ (2 marks)

24(c) $\dfrac{100!}{98!}$

Answer................................ (2 marks)

25 Look at the diagram.

Find the size of angle x.

140°   80°

Answer................................ (2 marks)

26   *A* is the point (5,6). *AB* and *BC* are two sides of a quadrilateral *ABCD* which has the dotted line as a line of symmetry.

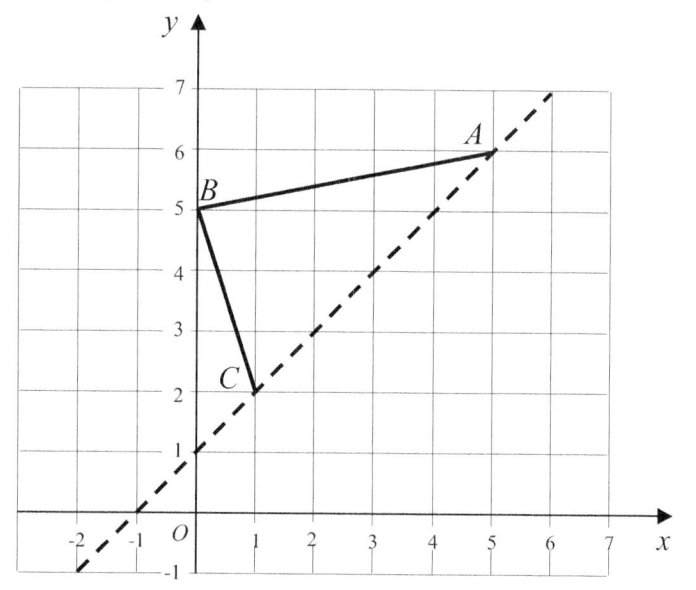

26(a)   Write down the coordinates of *B* and *C*.

....

....

....

       Answer................................   (2 marks)

26(b)   On the diagram, draw the sides *CD* and *AD* of the quadrilateral, and write down the coordinates of *D*.

....

....

....

       Answer................................   (2 marks)

26(c)   Write down the name of the quadrilateral *ABCD*.

....

....

....

       Answer................................   (2 marks)

27   The diagram below is made from three squares.

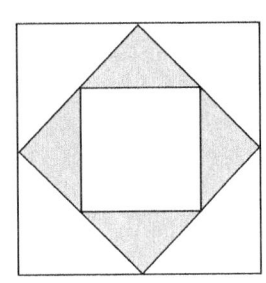

Work out the fraction of the larger square that is shaded.

Give your answer in the simplest form.

Answer............................ (3 marks)

28   It takes a team of four people six hours to paint my fence.

28(a) How long would a team of eight people have taken?

Answer............................ (2 marks)

28(b) One of my neighbours has a similar fence which is twice as long as mine.

She would like the work to be completed in less than five hours.

What is the minimum number of people that she should employ?

Answer............................ (3 marks)

29 The diagram shows a circle with a diameter, *AB*. The point *A* has coordinates (4, 3).
The centre has coordinates (8, 7).
Work out the coordinates of the point at the other end of the diameter, *B*.

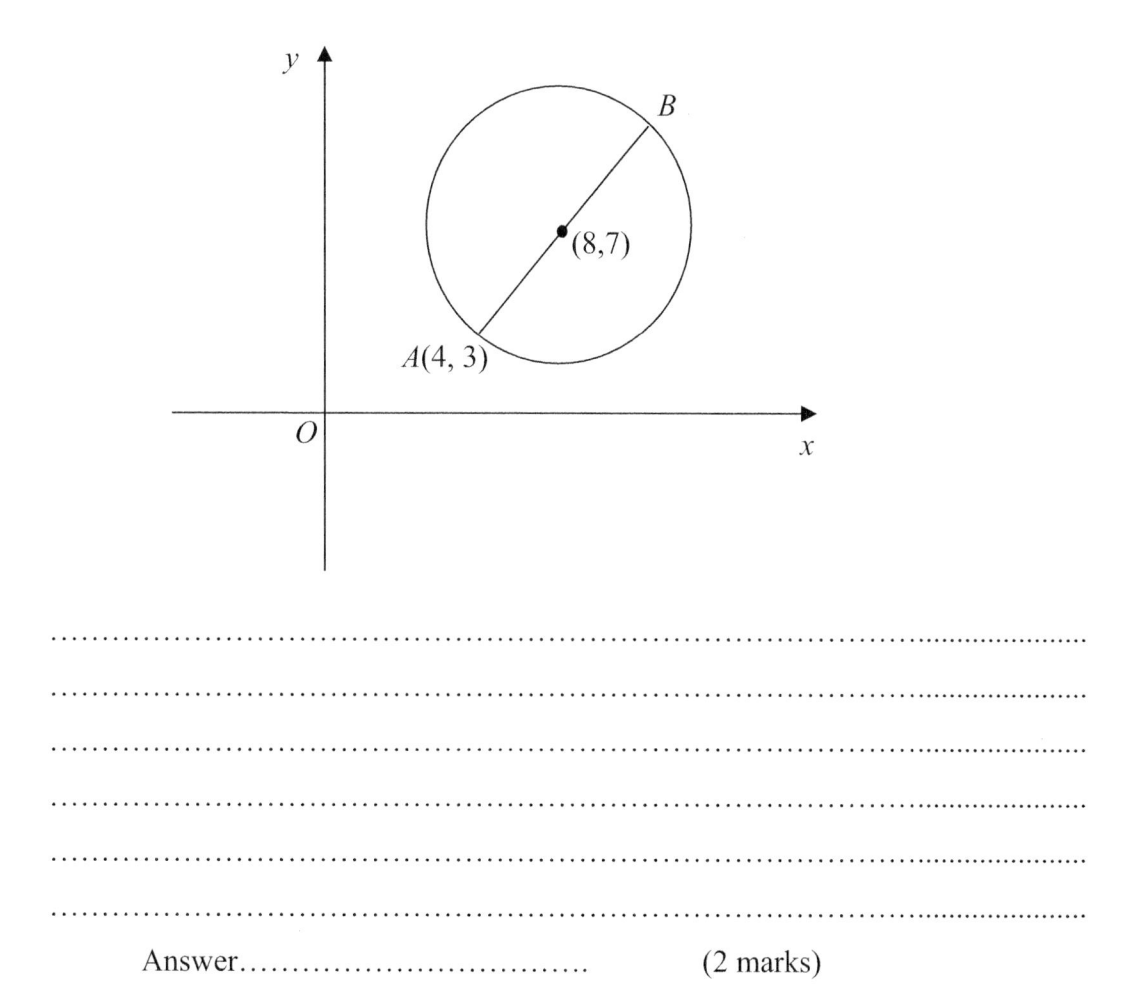

....
....
....
....
....
....

Answer.............................. (2 marks)

30(a) Write the correct number in each box.

```
        3  ☐
    ×      ☐
    ─────────
        2 5 9
    ─────────
```

(2 marks)

....
....
....

4

30(b) Can you find numbers to replace A, B and C in this sum?

(A, B and C are all different numbers)

```
    A B C
    A B C
+   A B C
  ———————
    B B B
```

....
....
....

Answer................................ (3 marks)

Paper 6

Materials
For this paper you must have:
- Pen, pencil, eraser and ruler.

Time allowed
1 hour.

Instructions
- Aim to complete as much as you can in the time given, without making mistakes.
- You must answer the questions in the space provided.
- Show all your working. You may be awarded marks for correct working even if your final answer is incorrect, and a correct answer unsupported by correct working may not receive full marks.
- Diagrams are not accurately drawn, unless otherwise indicated.
- Calculators are **NOT** allowed.

Information
- There are 30 questions on this paper
- The marks for questions are shown in brackets.
- The maximum mark is 100.

Advice
- Read each question carefully before you start to answer it.
- Keep an eye on the time.
- Don't worry if you don't complete the paper. If you get stuck, just go on to the next question and if you have time at the end come back to the one(s) you left.

1   Circle the highest number in each group.

1(a)   0.609   0.069   0.63   0.063

....
....

          Answer................................   (2 marks)

1(b)   -7.5   -1   -8   -1.5

....
....

          Answer................................   (2 marks)

1(c)   0.09 $\frac{39}{100}$ 0.44 $\frac{2}{5}$

....
....

          Answer................................   (2 marks)

2   Write down the next two terms in each of the following sequences:

2(a) $\frac{1}{2}$, $\frac{1}{4}$, $\frac{1}{8}$, ..., ...

....
....
....

          Answer................................   (2 marks)

2(b)   10.25,   10.50,   10.75, ..., ...,

....
....
....

          Answer................................   (2 marks)

3   Write down all the numbers smaller than 100 which are multiples of both 6 and 8.

    ....
    ....
    ....
    ....

                Answer................................   (2 marks)

4   Find the highest common factor (HCF) of 15, 30 and 45

    ....
    ....
    ....

                Answer................................   (2 marks)

5   One third of the pupils in a class are girls. The rest are boys. What is the ratio of girls to boys?

    Circle your answer.

    1:1   1:2   1:3   1:4   1:5

    ....
    ....
    ....

                Answer................................   (2 marks)

6   Arrange the following fractions in numerical size order, starting with the smallest order.

    $\frac{4}{7}$ $\frac{1}{5}$ $\frac{3}{8}$ $\frac{1}{6}$ $\frac{1}{10}$

    ....
    ....
    ....

                                                              (2 marks)

8

7   Write each percentage as a fraction in its simplest form:

7(a)   30%

Answer.................................   (2 marks)

7(b)   5%

Answer.................................   (2 marks)

7(c) $66\frac{2}{3}\%$

Answer.................................   (2 marks)

7(d)   120%

Answer.................................   (2 marks)

8   This is Jack's function machine.

? → [Subtract 10] → [Divide by 9] → 8

What number did he start with?

Answer.................................   (2 marks)

9 Round each of the following numbers to the accuracy given in brackets.

9(a) 18.52 (nearest whole number)

....

....

Answer................................ (2 marks)

9(b) 120550 (nearest thousand)

....

....

Answer................................ (2 marks)

9(c) 26.45789 (nearest tenth)

....

....

Answer................................ (2 marks)

10 In the square below, every row, column and diagonal adds up to 30.

Fill the remaining squares with numbers obeying this rule.

12		
	10	
16		

....

....

(2 marks)

11 Jack thinks of a whole number, rounds it to the nearest 100 and gets an answer of 500.

11(a) What is the smallest number that Jack might have thought of?

....

....

Answer................................ (2 marks)

11(b) What is the largest number that Jack might have thought of?

....

....

Answer................................ (2 marks)

12 A clothes shop has a sale. In the sale, normal prices are reduced by 10%.

12(a) The normal price of a tie is £9.00.

Work out the sale price of the tie.

....

....

....

Answer................................ (2 marks)

12(b) The price of a jacket is reduced by £12.00 in the sale.

Work out the normal price of the jacket.

....

....

....

Answer................................ (2 marks)

13 Mr and Mrs Smith take their 3 children to a cinema to watch a film. Tickets cost £8.00 each for adults. The price of a child's ticket is half that of an adult's.

How much does it cost the family to watch the film in the cinema?

....

....

....

Answer................................ (2 marks)

14 This shape has been created using two identical isosceles triangles ABC and CDE.

∠A = ∠E = 30°

Work out the value of ∠ACE

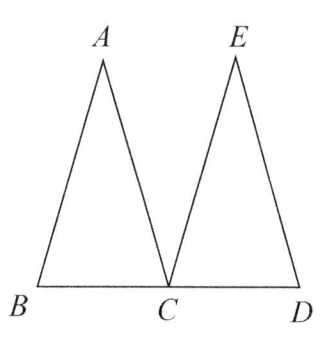

....
....
....

Answer.............................. (2 marks)

15 Here is an L-shape. All lengths are in centimetres.

Work out the area of the shape.

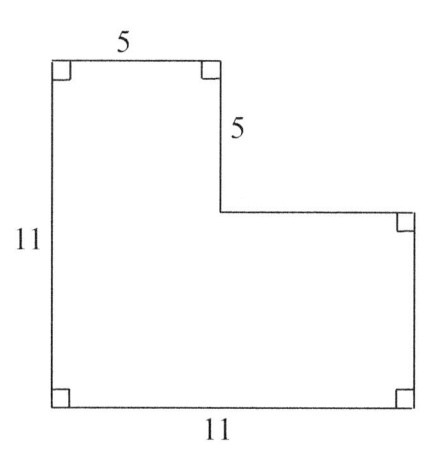

....
....
....

Answer.............................. (2 marks)

16. Shape A and shape B are each made from nine identical squares. The perimeter of shape A is 72 cm. Work out the perimeter of shape B.

A

B

Answer…………………………….   (3 marks)

17. The pie chart shows the proportions of different drinks chosen from a machine in one day. There were 15 cartons of orange juice taken. How many cartons of pineapple juice were taken?

Orange 12.5%
Apple 37.5%
Blackcurrant 20%
Pineapple

Answer…………………………….   (3 marks)

18   *ABCD* is a kite.

   Write down the coordinates of vertex *D*.

   ....
   ....
   ....

   Answer............................... (3 marks)

19   On Christmas Eve, the temperature in Beijing was −14°C.

   At the same time, the temperature in Sydney was 18°C.

19(a) How many degrees hotter was it in Sydney than in Beijing?

   ....
   ....
   ....

   Answer............................... (2 marks)

19(b) By Christmas Day, the temperature in Beijing had risen by 5°C.

   What was the temperature in Beijing on Christmas Day?

   ....
   ....
   ....

   Answer............................... (2 marks)

20   The diagram below shows a shaded parallelogram drawn inside a rectangle.
     Work out the area of the shaded parallelogram

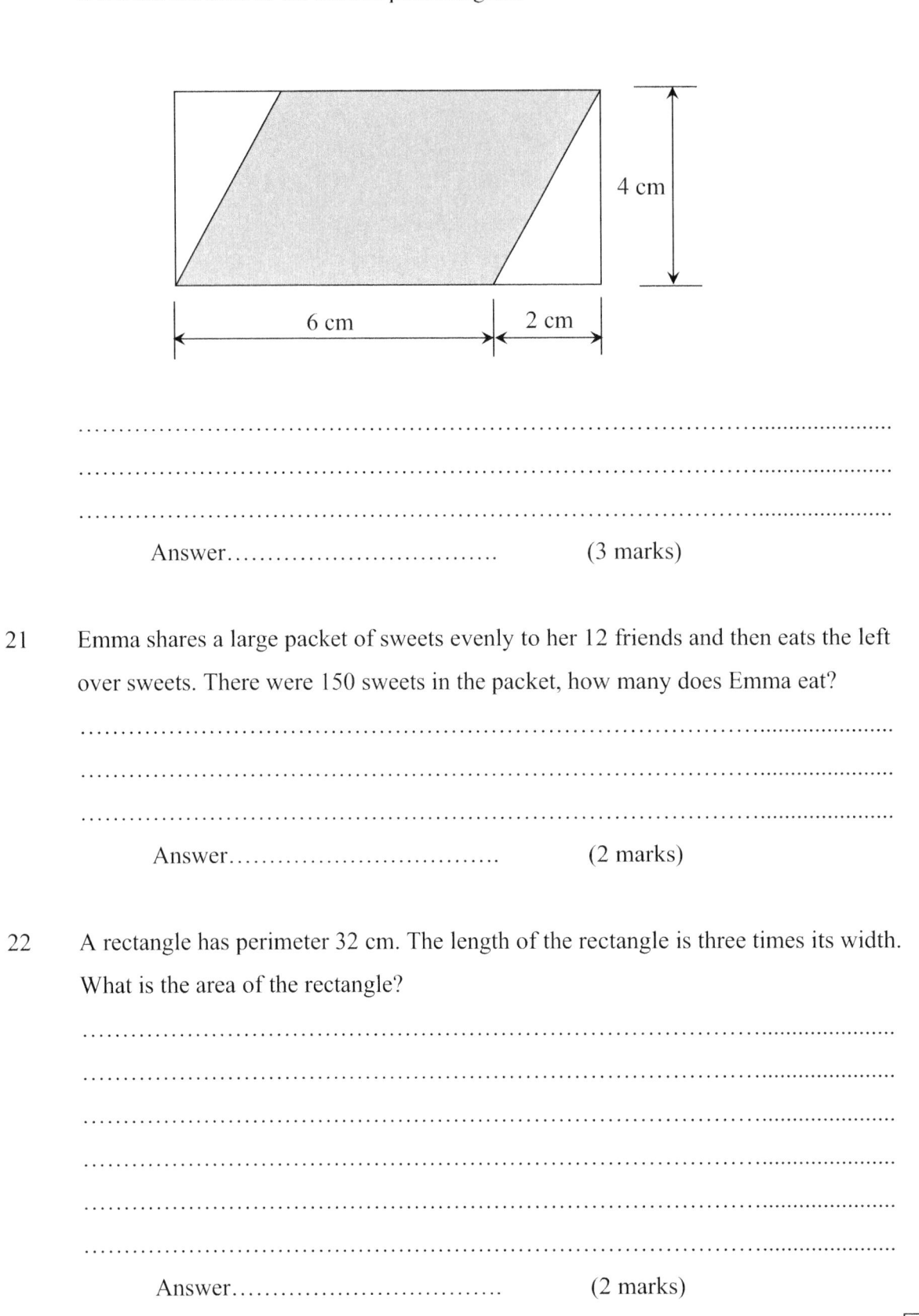

     4 cm
     6 cm   2 cm

     Answer…………………………..   (3 marks)

21   Emma shares a large packet of sweets evenly to her 12 friends and then eats the left over sweets. There were 150 sweets in the packet, how many does Emma eat?

     Answer…………………………..   (2 marks)

22   A rectangle has perimeter 32 cm. The length of the rectangle is three times its width. What is the area of the rectangle?

     Answer…………………………..   (2 marks)

23 A pattern is made from two identical squares.

The sides of the squares are parallel to the axes.

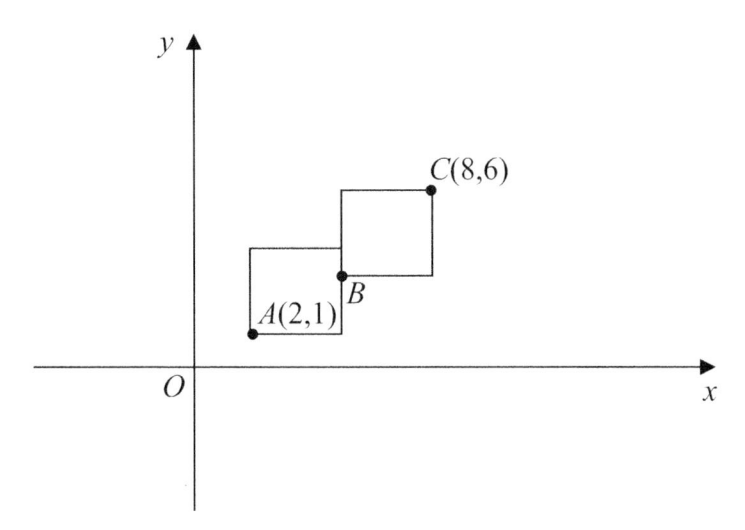

Point A has coordinates $(2, 1)$

Point C has coordinates $(8, 6)$

Point B is marked on the diagram.

Work out the coordinates of B.

Answer.............................. (4 marks)

24(a) On the diagram, draw the image of Shape A when it is reflected in the *x*-axis.

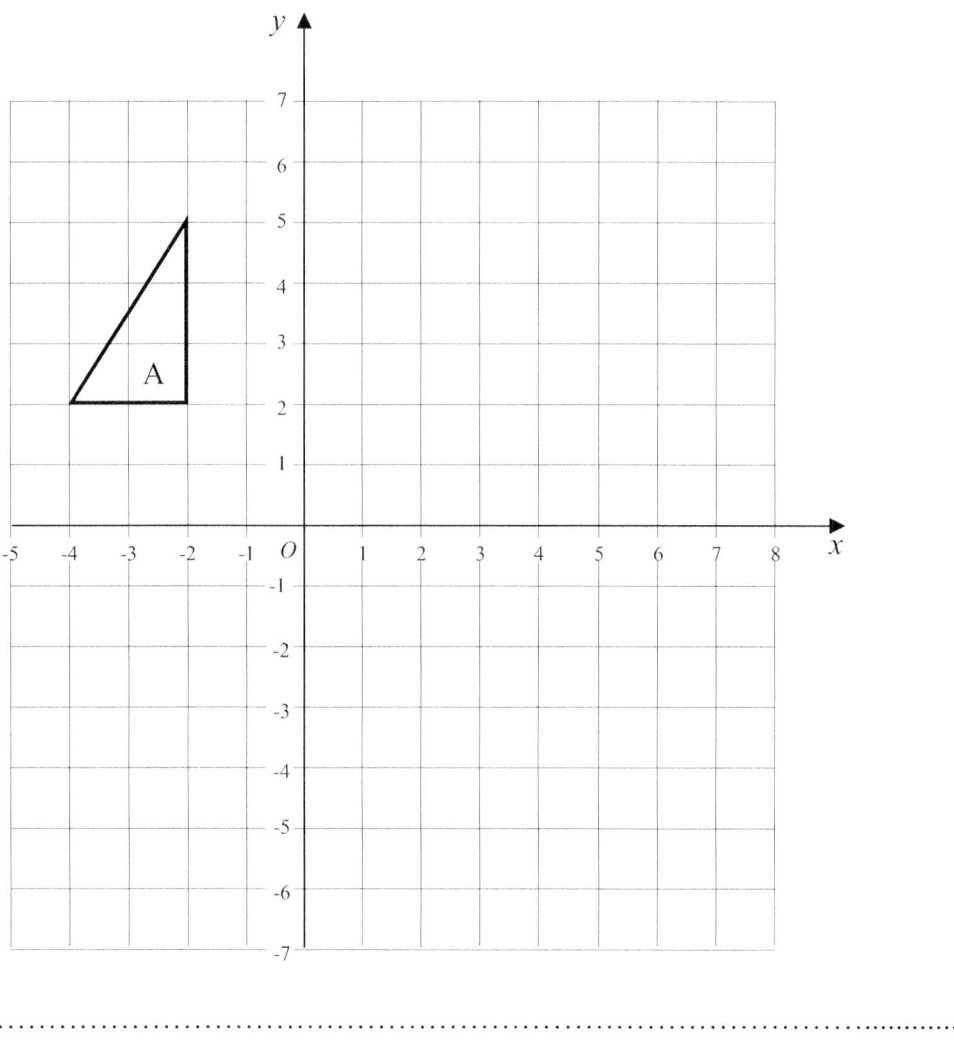

....
....

(2 marks)

24(b) On the diagram, draw the image of Shape A again when it is translated by 6 right and 1 down

....
....
....

(2 marks)

25   Emma is choosing pairs of numbers from this list.

    4   23   45   58   120

25(a) She multiplies two numbers together.

Which two numbers should she choose to get an answer between 200 and 300?

....

....

....

        Answer................................   (2 marks)

25(b) Which two numbers have the highest common factor (HCF)?

....

....

....

        Answer................................   (3 marks)

26   The table shows Ann's marks in two tests.

Test	Mark
1	60 out of 80
2	70 out of 100

In which test did Ann do better?

You **must** show your working.

....

....

....

        Answer................................   (3 marks)

27   Jack is 30 years older than Mark. In 18 years Jack will be twice Mark's age. How old is Mark?

....

....

....

        Answer................................   (3 marks)

28 The sum of five consecutive whole numbers is 75.

What is the smallest of these five numbers?

....

....

....

Answer................................ (3 marks)

29 I flip a fair coin that has the number 3 on one side and the number 7 on the other side. At the same time I roll a fair six sided die that has the numbers 1 to 6 on it. Then I add the two numbers. If I do this 60 times how many times would you expect me to get a total of 7?

....

....

....

....

....

....

Answer................................ (3 marks)

30(a) In this multiplication, each letter stands for a different digit. What digit does C represent? Show your working.

```
    A 6 B 4
  ×       7
  ---------
  C 6 D 9 8
```

....

....

....

Answer................................ (2 marks)

30(b) A, B and C are all different numbers.

Can you find numbers to replace A, B and C in this sum?

$$\begin{array}{r} A \\ A \\ +\ \ B\ B \\ \hline C\ C\ C \\ \hline \end{array}$$

....
....
....

Answer............................ (3 marks)

Paper 7

Materials
For this paper you must have:
- Pen, pencil, eraser and ruler.

Time allowed
1 hour.

Instructions
- Aim to complete as much as you can in the time given, without making mistakes.
- You must answer the questions in the space provided.
- Show all your working. You may be awarded marks for correct working even if your final answer is incorrect, and a correct answer unsupported by correct working may not receive full marks.
- Diagrams are not accurately drawn, unless otherwise indicated.
- Calculators are **NOT** allowed.

Information
- There are 30 questions on this paper
- The marks for questions are shown in brackets.
- The maximum mark is 100.

Advice
- Read each question carefully before you start to answer it.
- Keep an eye on the time.
- Don't worry if you don't complete the paper. If you get stuck, just go on to the next question and if you have time at the end come back to the one(s) you left.

1 Work out the missing values

1(a) 11% of 3600 = ...

....

....

Answer................................ (2 marks)

1(b) .... % of 52 = 13

....

....

Answer................................ (2 marks)

1(c) 15 % of .... = 60

....

....

Answer................................ (2 marks)

2(a) Calculate 50% of 20% of 5000

....

....

Answer................................ (2 marks)

2(b) Calculate 20192019 ÷ 2019

....

....

....

....

....

....

Answer................................ (2 marks)

3   Emma correctly worked out that 2451 ÷ 43 = 57.

3(a)   What is the value of 43 × 57 + 9 ?

....

....

Answer................................   (2 marks)

3(b)   What is the value of 2.451 ÷ 0.43?

....

....

Answer................................   (2 marks)

4   The ratio of flour to sugar in a cake is 11 : 4.

If 200 grams of sugar was used to make the cake, how much flour was used?

....

....

Answer................................   (2 marks)

5   Write these decimals in order of size, starting with the smallest:

2.3   2.23   2.303   2.203

....

....

....

Answer................................   (2 marks)

6   Emma buys a pair of jeans.

20% VAT is added to the price of the jeans.

Emma has to pay a total of £60.

What is the price of the jeans with **no** VAT added?

....

....

....

Answer................................   (2 marks)

7   The students on a Geography trip to Iceland arrive at Heathrow Airport at 10:45.

Their flight leaves at 13:05.

How many minutes do they have to wait at the airport before their flight leaves?

....

....

Answer……………………………….   (2 marks)

8   The table shows the technology subjects studies by a group of students.

	Art	Design Tech	Textiles	Total
Boys	23		0	60
Girls		14	6	
Total	53		6	

Complete the table above.

....

....

(3 marks)

9   Jack paid a £50 deposit for a TV, then monthly payments of £25 each. The TV cost £550.

How many monthly payments did Jack have to make to buy it?

....

....

....

Answer……………………………….   (2 marks)

10   There are 600 pupils at Jack's school. There are 50 more girls than boys.

How many girls are there?

....

....

....

Answer……………………………….   (2 marks)

11 MAGNUM washing-up liquid is sold in two quantities, 500 ml and 250 ml. They cost £1.05 and 60 p respectively.

Which of these two quantities is the better value for money?

....

....

....

....

Answer................................ (2 marks)

12 Match the following numbers to the labelled points on the number line.

1·796   1·799   1·776   1·792   1·814   1·782

12(a) 1·796 is matched with .... (2 marks)

....

12(b) 1·799 is matched with .... (2 marks)

....

12(c) 1·776 is matched with .... (2 marks)

....

12(d) 1·792 is matched with .... (2 marks)

....

12(e) 1·814 is matched with .... (2 marks)

....

12(f) 1·782 is matched with .... (2 marks)

....

13. The difference between $\frac{1}{4}$ of a number and $\frac{1}{5}$ of the same number is 5.

What is the number?

Answer…………………………. (2 marks)

14. Kate takes one a day of each of two types of tablet. One type of tablet is in packets of 15 and the other type is in packets of 20. She starts new packets of both on 1st March.

On what date will she next start new packets of both?

Answer…………………………. (3 marks)

15. Anna decides to share her pizza with two of her friends. She gives one friend a fifth of the pizza and the other friend three tenths of the pizza.

What fraction of the pizza is left for Anna?

Answer…………………………. (2 marks)

16   Mr Fryer and his sons Jack and Mark have the same birthday. Today, Mr Fryer is 38, Jack is 10 and Mark is 7.

How old will they be when Mr Fryer's age is the sum of his sons' ages?

Mr Fryer ……………years

Jack ……………years

Mark ……………years

………………………………………………………………………………………………

………………………………………………………………………………………………

………………………………………………………………………………………………

………………………………………………………………………………………………

………………………………………………………………………………………………

………………………………………………………………………………………………

(3 marks)

17   Three boxes (A, B and C) contain red balls or yellow balls or both.

Each box contains the same number of balls.

Box A contains all twelve of the red balls and one ninth of the yellow balls.

17(a)   How many yellow balls are there altogether?

………………………………………………………………………………………………

………………………………………………………………………………………………

………………………………………………………………………………………………

………………………………………………………………………………………………

Answer……………………….   (2 marks)

17(b)   How many balls are there in each box?

………………………………………………………………………………………………

………………………………………………………………………………………………

………………………………………………………………………………………………

Answer…………………….   (2 marks)

7

18   Emma has 6 equilateral triangles, each with a perimeter of 15 cm. She fits them together to make a regular hexagon.

Work out the perimeter of the hexagon.

Answer............................... (3 marks)

19   Jack has 4 equilateral triangles, each with a perimeter of 15 cm. He fits them together to make a larger equilateral triangle.

Work out the perimeter of the larger equilateral triangle.

Answer............................... (3 marks)

20   Here are triangles.

Work out the values of a and b.

Answer............................... (2 marks)

21 40 people were asked to choose a drink.

One quarter chose tea. Three eighths of them chose coffee. 30% of them chose orange juice. The rest chose water.

21(a) How many people chose water?

....
....
....

Answer............................ (2 marks)

21(b) Emma drew a pie chart to show all their choices.

How many degrees should 'Water' have on her pie chart?

....
....
....

Answer............................ (2 marks)

22 Here are four cards.

| 1 | 5 | 3 | 4 |

22(a) Choose two cards to make a two-digit multiple of 6.

....
....
....

Answer............................ (2 marks)

22(b) Choose two cards to make a two-digit factor of 65.

....
....
....

Answer............................ (2 marks)

23 Jack picks one of these cards at random.

| 1 | 2 | 3 | 4 | 5 | 6 | 7 | 8 | 9 |

Here are some possible outcomes.

A   The number on the card will be a factor of 12.
B   The number on the card will be a multiple of 2.
C   The number on the card will be a multiple of 3.
D   The number on the card will be a multiple of 4.
E   The number on the card will be a square number.

23(a) Which of these outcomes (A, B, C, D, E) is the most likely to happen?

....
....
....
....
....

Answer……………………………….   (2 marks)

23(b) Which of these outcomes (A, B, C, D, E) is the least likely to happen?

....
....
....
....
....

Answer……………………………….   (2 marks)

23(c) Which two of these outcomes (A, B, C, D, E) are equally likely to happen?

....
....
....
....
....

Answer……………………………….   (2 marks)

24 In this partly completed pyramid, each rectangle is to be filled with the sum of the numbers in the two triangles just below it.

Which number should replace *x*?

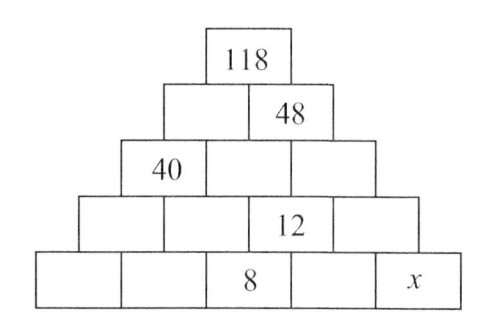

			118			
				48		
	40					
			12			
		8			*x*	

....

....

....

Answer…………………………….   (3 marks)

25 Here is a regular octagon.

Shade in $\frac{3}{4}$ of this shape

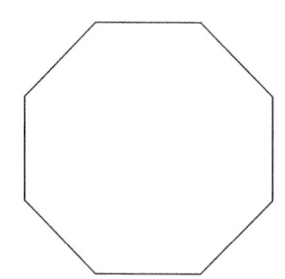

....

....

....

....

....

....

(3 marks)

26 This diagram shows a regular hexagon.

    What fraction of the hexagon is shaded?

    ....
    ....
    ....
    ....
    ....
    ....

         Answer................................   (3 marks)

27 Work out the number from the following clues:

    A   It is a whole number.
    B   It is less than 80.
    C   It is square number.
    D   It is one more than a multiple of 5.
    E   3 is a factor of this number.

    ....
    ....
    ....
    ....
    ....
    ....

         Answer................................   (3 marks)

28 You are told that $121 \times 121 = 14641$

Use this fact and the idea above to work out the value of 119×123. (Note: Do not multiply 119 by 123)

....
....
....

Answer............................ (3 marks)

29 Emma spent $\frac{1}{3}$ of her money on a new top and $\frac{1}{3}$ of the remainder on a skirt. She had £8 left. How much did Emma spend altogether?

....
....
....
....
....
....

Answer............................ (3 marks)

30 A cuboid has faces with areas of 40 cm², 55 cm² and 88 cm². What are the lengths of its sides?

....
....
....
....
....
....

Answer............................ (3 marks)

Paper 8

Materials

For this paper you must have:
- Pen, pencil, eraser and ruler.

Time allowed

1 hour.

Instructions
- Aim to complete as much as you can in the time given, without making mistakes.
- You must answer the questions in the space provided.
- Show all your working. You may be awarded marks for correct working even if your final answer is incorrect, and a correct answer unsupported by correct working may not receive full marks.
- Diagrams are not accurately drawn, unless otherwise indicated.
- Calculators are **NOT** allowed.

Information
- There are 30 questions on this paper
- The marks for questions are shown in brackets.
- The maximum mark is 100.

Advice
- Read each question carefully before you start to answer it.
- Keep an eye on the time.
- Don't worry if you don't complete the paper. If you get stuck, just go on to the next question and if you have time at the end come back to the one(s) you left.

1   You are told that $12 \times 1284 = 15408$

Use this answer to work out the values of:

1(a) 6×1284

Answer.................................. (2 marks)

1(b) 24×128.4

Answer.................................. (2 marks)

2(a) 360×19 is more than 350×19

How much more?

Answer.................................. (2 marks)

2(b)   Work out the product of 499 and 99.

Answer.................................. (2 marks)

3(a)   Find 15% of 240

Answer.................................. (2 marks)

3(b) Find the difference between 10% of £20 and 20% of £10.

Answer................................ (2 marks)

3(c) What is five sevenths of 707?

Answer................................ (2 marks)

4 Which fraction is half way between $\frac{1}{7}$ and $\frac{1}{3}$

Give your answer in its simplest form.

Answer................................ (2 marks)

5 Change 0.36 to a fraction

Give your answer in its simplest form.

Answer................................ (2 marks)

6 Two numbers have a sum of 11 and a product of 24. What is their difference?

Answer................................ (3 marks)

11

7   Arrange the numbers, 5, 4, 9 and 2 to make the largest possible four-digit number which is a multiple of 5.

    ....
    ....

        Answer................................   (3 marks)

8   If it is -26.5°C in Canada and 34.5°C in Australia, what is the difference in temperature?

    ....
    ....

        Answer................................   (3 marks)

9   Write down (in simplest form) the fraction that the arrow is pointing to.

    ....
    ....

        Answer................................   (3 marks)

10   What is the size of angle "*a*"?

    ....
    ....
    ....
    ....
    ....

        Answer................................   (3 marks)

11 Here is diagram. $AB = AC$. Work out the values of x and y.

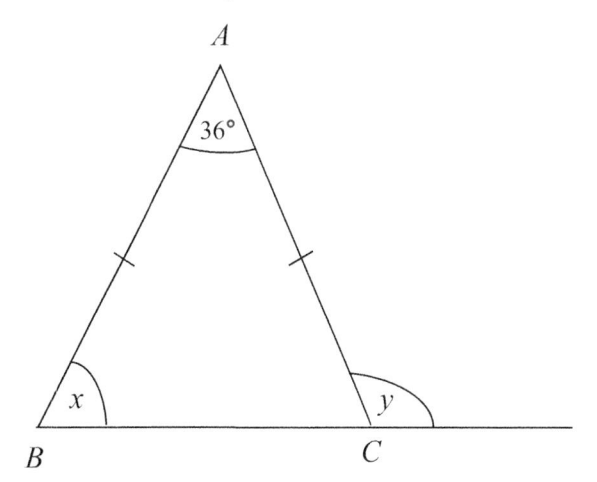

....

....

....

Answer…………………………. (3 marks)

12 Shade 44% of this shape.

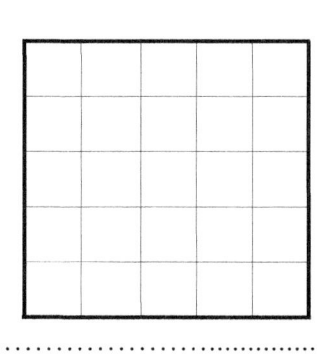

....

....

....

(3 marks)

13   Find the area of the following shaded shapes.

   Scale: 1 square = 1 cm²

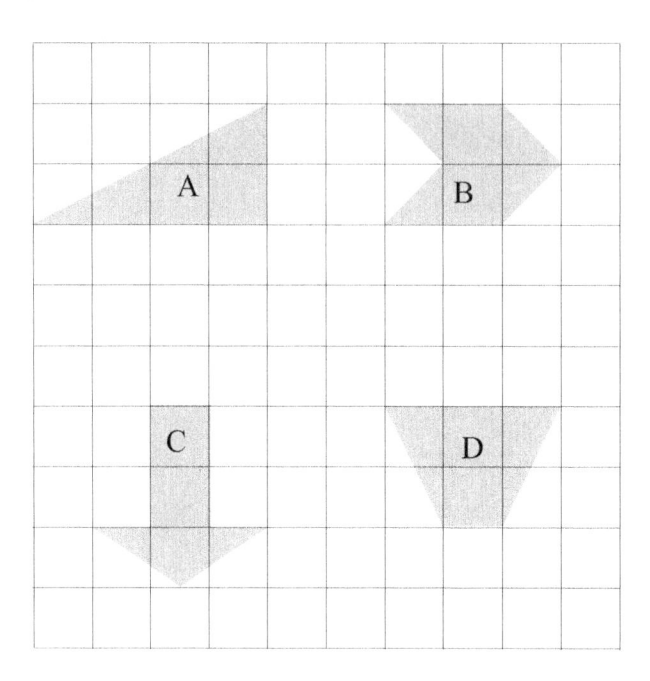

   ....
   ....
   ....
   ....

         Answer................................   (4 marks)

14   Here is a straight-line graph.

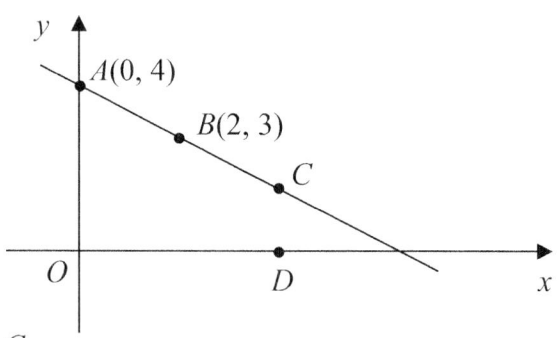

   Point B is the midpoint of points A and C.

14(a)   What are the coordinates of point C?

   ....
   ....
   ....
   ....

         Answer................................   (3 marks)

14(b)   Point *D* is directly below point *C* as shown.

What are the coordinates of point *D*?

....

....

....

Answer……………………….   (3 marks)

15   I want to cut out a circle of radius 5.5 cm from a square piece of card.

What is the area of the smallest square I can use?

....

....

....

Answer……………………….   (3 marks)

16   Four bells ring at intervals of 2, 6, 9 and 12 seconds.

If they are all rung at the same time, how many seconds will pass before they all ring at the same time again?

....

....

....

....

Answer……………………….   (3 marks)

17   When my age is divided by 2, 3, 4 or 6, there is always a remainder of 1. But when divided by 5 there is no remainder. I am less than 50 years old.

How old am I?

....

....

....

....

Answer……………………….   (3 marks)

18   I opened a book at random and multiplied the two page numbers together.

The answer was 156. What were the numbers on the two pages?

....

....

....

Answer.............................. (3 marks)

19   Bill, Mark, Jack, Alex and Emma went to the cinema. They spent £30 on tickets and £20·50 on food. They shared the cost equally.

How much did each have to pay?

....

....

....

Answer.............................. (3 marks)

20   A street has forty six houses, door plate numbers are from 1 to 46.

How many digit 2s are used on the complete set of door plates for this street?

....

....

....

....

....

....

Answer.............................. (3 marks)

21   In Beijing China the time is 8 hours ahead of the UK. Emma decides to phone her Great Aunt Maria at 23:00 UK time on the 30th January.

What is the time and date in Beijing when Maria receives the call?

....

....

....

Answer.............................. (3 marks)

12

22   Of the 30 boys in a class, 28 are right-handed. If 10 of the boys in the class wear glasses.

What is the minimum number of boys in the class who are both right-handed and wear glasses?

....

....

....

....

....

....

....

....

Answer……………………….   (3 marks)

23   Emma, Jack and Mark share some money. Emma gets £10 more than Jack, Jack gets £15 more than Mark. The total amount of the money is £100.

How much does Mark get?

....

....

....

Answer……………………….   (3 marks)

24   What is the angle between the hands of a clock at half past ten?

   Answer……………………….   (3 marks)

25   On the 1st January 2016 my grandmother was 80 years old. Her daughter was 40 years old on the 1st January 2004. How old was my grandmother when her daughter was born?

   Answer……………………….   (3 marks)

26   Jack's bucket weighs 20 kg when full of water. After he pours half the water from the bucket, it weighs 13 kg.
   What is the weight of the empty bucket?

   Answer……………………….   (3 marks)

27 In a barn there are only horses and hens. If they have 60 heads and 140 legs in total, how many horses and how many hens are there?

....
....
....
....
....

Answer............................... (3 marks)

28 A number of children are standing in a circle. They are evenly spaced and the 6th child is directly opposite the 17th child. How many children are there altogether?

....
....
....
....
....
....

Answer............................... (3 marks)

29 Jack and Mark are having a race. Jack starts running from the start line at 10m/s. Three seconds later Mark starts running from the start line at 12m/s.

29(a) How long after Jack starts running does Mark catch up with him?

....
....
....

Answer............................... (3 marks)

29(b) How far are they both from the start line when Mark catches up with Jack?

....
....
....

Answer............................... (2 marks)

11

30   Write the correct digit in each box.

30(a)

```
    1  1  1  ☐
  -    ☐  1  1
  ─────────────
       1  ☐  ☐
```

....
....
....

(2 marks)

30(b)

```
         6 ☐ ☐
      ┌─────────
    7 │ ☐ 4 ☐ 4
```

....
....
....

(2 marks)

Paper 5 solutions

1 Work out the following:

1(a) $32 - 6 \times 3 + 12$

$32 - 6 \times 3 + 12 = 32 - 18 + 12 = 14 + 12 = 26$

Answer   26   (1 mark)

1(b) $9^2 - 8^2$

$9^2 - 8^2 = 81 - 64 = 17$

Answer   17   (1 mark)

1(c) $11^2 - 9^2$

$11^2 - 9^2 = 121 - 81 = 40$

Answer   40   (1 mark)

1(d) $4 \div 0.02$

$4 \div 0.02 = 4 \times 100 \div 2 = 400 \div 2 = 200$

Answer   200   (1 mark)

2 What number is:

2(a) Six less than -10

$-10 - 6 = -16$

Answer   -16   (1 mark)

2(b) Twelve more than -8

$-8 + 12 = 4$

Answer   4   (1 mark)

3(a) What is 30% of 40?

$30\% \times 40 = 12$

Answer   12   (1 mark)

7

3(b)   What is $\frac{2}{3}$ of 81

$$\frac{2}{\cancel{3}_1} \times \cancel{81}^{27} = 54$$

    Answer   54   (1 mark)

4 Calculate how much bigger $3\frac{1}{2}$ is than $1\frac{3}{4}$

Give your answer as a decimal.

$$3\frac{1}{2} - 1\frac{3}{4} = 3\frac{2}{4} - 1\frac{3}{4} = 2\frac{6}{4} - 1\frac{3}{4} = 1\frac{3}{4} = 1.75$$

    Answer   1.75   (2 marks)

5 The sums below were correct before someone rubbed out the brackets. Write down the correct sums, including the brackets.

5(a) $9 - 6 + 4 = -1$ (1 mark)

   $9 - (6 + 4) = -1$

5(b) $11 - 12 + 3 - 4 = 0$ (1 mark)

   $11 - (12 + 3 - 4) = 0$

6 The distance from Calais to Paris is 200 miles.

5 miles is approximately 8 kilometres.

Calculate the approximate distance in kilometres from Calais to Paris.

$$\frac{200}{5} \times 8 = 320$$

    Answer   320 km   (2 marks)

7

7   Here are the numbers of music CDs which the 6 students had.

Name	Jack	Emma	Lucy	Mark	Kath	Sam
Number	5	7	15	19	15	11

7(a)   What is the mode?

"15" appears most often.

   Answer   15   (2 marks)

7(b)   What is the median?

$$\frac{11+15}{2} = 13$$

   Answer   13   (2 marks)

7(c)   What is the range?

$19 - 5 = 14$

   Answer   14   (2 marks)

7(d)   What is the mean?

$$\frac{5+7+11+15+15+19}{6} = 12$$

   Answer   12   (2 marks)

8   Write down the next two terms in each of the following sequences:

8(a)   6, 12, 18, 24, ..., ...

6, 12, 18, 24, 30, 36

   Answer   30, 36   (2 marks)

8(b)   60, 52, 44, 36, ..., ...

60, 52, 44, 36, 28, 20

   Answer   28, 20   (2 marks)

8(c) 2, 4, 8, 16, ... , ...

  2, 4, 8, 16, 32, 64

  Answer   32, 64   (2 marks)

8(d) 10, 22, 32, 40, ... , ...

  10, 22, 32, 40, 46, 50

  Answer   46, 50   (2 marks)

9 Place the following numbers in descending order:

  $\dfrac{4}{5}$ 0.6 $\dfrac{3}{4}$ 0.7 $\dfrac{2}{3}$

  $\dfrac{4}{5} = 0.8$, $\dfrac{3}{4} = 0.75$, $\dfrac{2}{3} \approx 0.667$

  Numbers in descending order are:

  $\dfrac{4}{5}$ $\dfrac{3}{4}$ 0.7 $\dfrac{2}{3}$ 0.6

  Answer $\dfrac{4}{5}$ $\dfrac{3}{4}$ 0.7 $\dfrac{2}{3}$ 0.6

  (2 marks)

10 Write down two numbers that add to 15 and multiply to 54.

  $54 = 7 \times 8$, $7 + 8 = 15$

  Answer   7 and 8   (2 marks)

11 A box holds 6 cakes. How many boxes are needed to store 75 cakes?

  $\dfrac{75}{6} = 12.5$

  ∴ 13 boxes are needed.

  Answer   13   (2 marks)

12 Which volume can give the best estimate of the capacity of a tea cup?

Circle your answer.

0.25 litres   0.5 litres   0.75 litres   1 litre   1.25 litres

(0.25 litres)   0.5 litres   0.75 litres   1 litre   1.25 litres

Answer   0.25 litres   (2 marks)

13 You are given the number 3975. You are allowed to swap the position of any two digits.

13(a) What is the largest possible number you can make using one swap?

Swap 3 and 9 to get 9375

Answer   9375   (2 marks)

13(b) What is the smallest possible number you can make using one swap?

Swap 5 and 9 to get 3579

Answer   3579   (2 marks)

14 Jack is 2 years and 8 months older than his sister Emma. Jack is 12 years and 6 months old.

How old is Emma?

12 years 6 months − 2 years 8 months = 11 years 18 months − 2 years 8 months = 9 years 10 months

Answer   9 years and 10 months old   (2 marks)

15 Children are offered a 25% discount on the cost of an adult ticket to see a film. Senior citizens are given a 20% discount.

If a child's ticket costs £30, how much does a senior citizen pay?

An adult ticket costs: $\frac{£30}{1-25\%} = £40$

A senior citizen ticket costs: $£40 \times (1-20\%) = £32$

Answer   £32   (2 marks)

16   The figure shows two identical overlapping triangles. Three sevenths of each triangle is shaded.
What fraction of the whole figure is shaded?

$$\frac{\frac{3}{7}}{\frac{3}{7}+\frac{4}{7}+\frac{4}{7}} = \frac{3}{11}$$

Answer $\frac{3}{11}$ (2 marks)

17   Jack and Emma start at the same point on the toy room floor and walk in opposite direction for 100 cm. Each then turns left and walks 80 cm. Finally each of them turns left again and walks 100 cm. How far apart are they then?
Their routes can be sketched as follows.

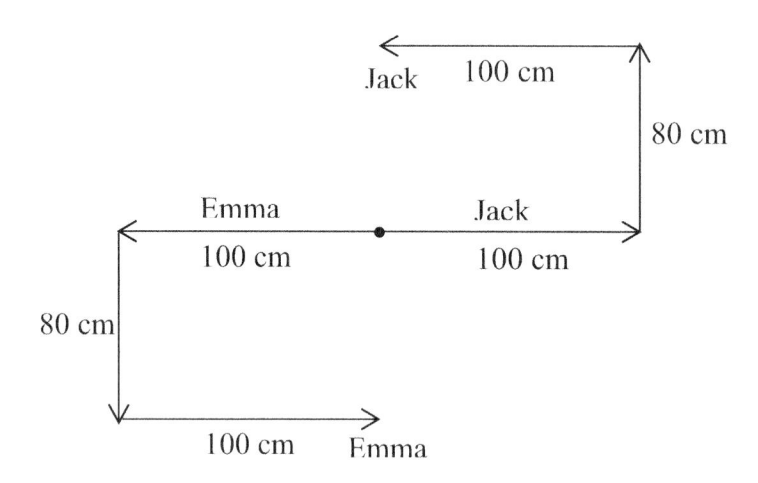

It is easy to see how far apart they are from the sketch: $80\,\text{cm} + 80\,\text{cm} = 160\,\text{cm}$

Answer   160 cm   (2 marks)

18 The pie chart shows data collected in a survey by a PE teacher about the favourite sports of a group of 96 school children. $\frac{1}{3}$ of the children preferred football.

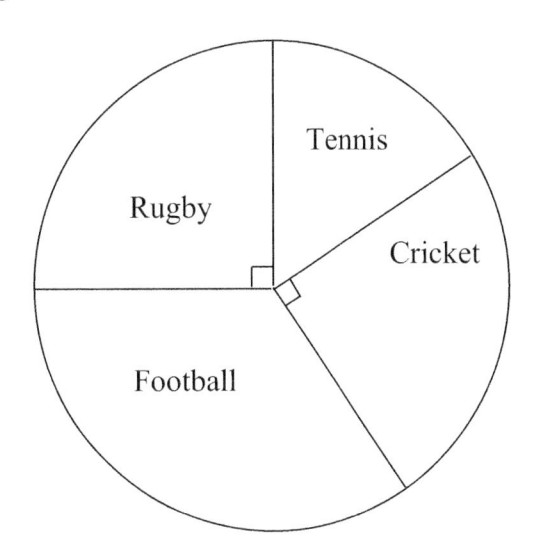

18(a) Work out the angle of the football sector.

$360° \times \frac{1}{3} = 120°$

Answer   120°   (2 marks)

18(b) Write down the fraction of the school children who liked tennis.

Give your answer in the simplest form.

The angle of the tennis sector is:

$360° - 120° - 90° - 90° = 60°$

$\frac{60°}{360°} = \frac{1}{6}$

Answer $\frac{1}{6}$ (2 marks)

18(c) How many children preferred Rugby?

The angle of Rugby sector is $90°$.

$\frac{90°}{360°} \times 96 = 24$

Answer   24   (2 marks)

20   This graph represents the journeys of a cyclist and a motorist. The motorist is faster than the cyclist.

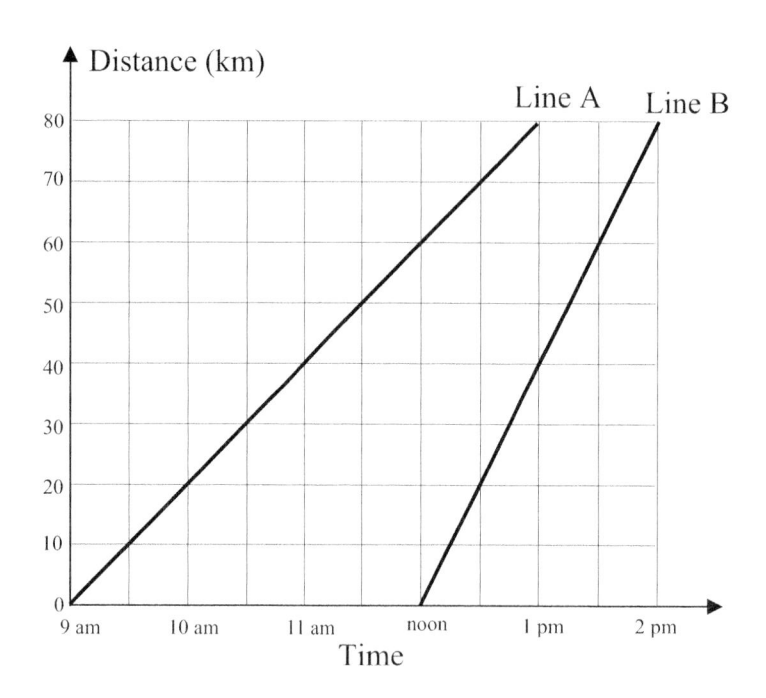

20(a)   Which line represents the journey of the motorist?

For Line A, it passed (9am, 0 km) and (1 pm, 80 km), and took 4 hours to travel 80 km, thus the speed is: $\dfrac{80\,\text{km}}{4\,\text{hr}} = 20\,\text{km/hr}$

For Line B, it passed (noon, 0 km) and (2 pm, 80 km), and took 2 hours to travel 80 km, thus the speed is: $\dfrac{80\,\text{km}}{2\,\text{hr}} = 40\,\text{km/hr}$

The motorist is faster than the cyclist. Line B represents the journey of the motorist.

Answer   Line B   (2 marks)

20(b)   At what speed was the cyclist travelling?

The speed of the cyclist travelling is 20 km/hr, from the calculation in part (a).

Answer   20 km/hr   (2 marks)

20(c)   At what speed was the motorist travelling?

The speed of the motorist travelling is 40 km/hr, from the calculation in part (a).

Answer   40 km/hr   (2 marks)

6

21 There are thirty pupils in a class. Ten pupils wear glasses. Sixteen pupils are girls. Of the sixteen girls, two wear glasses.

Enter this information into the table below. Then complete the rest of the table.

	Wear glasses	Not wear glasses	Total
Boys			
Girls	2		16
Total	10		30

(3 marks)

The completed table is as follow.

	Wear glasses	Not wear glasses	Total
Boys	8	6	14
Girls	2	14	16
Total	10	20	30

22 There are three numbers. One is a multiple of 14; and the other two are different factors of 55. The sum of the three numbers is greater than fifty but less than sixty. Work out the three numbers.

55 has the factors, 1, 5, 11 and 55.

The multiple of 14 could be, 14, 28, 42, 56, ……

The sum of the three numbers is greater than fifty but less than sixty.

Thus the three numbers are: 5, 11 and 42.

Answer   5, 11, 42   (3 marks)

23   This is a magic square.

All the columns, rows and diagonals add up to 15.

Several numbers have been missed out.

Fill the remaining squares with numbers obeying this rule.

		6
	5	1

(3 marks)

The completed magic square is as follows.

2	7	6
9	5	1
4	3	8

24   The notation 4! is used as an abbreviation for the product $4 \times 3 \times 2 \times 1$ so that $4! = 24$.

Similarly, $9! = 9 \times 8 \times 7 \times 6 \times 5 \times 4 \times 3 \times 2 \times 1 = 362880$.

Work out the value of

24(a)   5!

$5! = 5 \times 4! = 5 \times 24 = 120$

Answer   120   (2 marks)

24(b)   10!

$10! = 10 \times 9! = 10 \times 362880 = 3628800$

Answer   3628800   (2 marks)

7

24(c) $\dfrac{100!}{98!}$

$\dfrac{100!}{98!} = \dfrac{100 \times 99 \times 98!}{98!} = 100 \times 99 = 9900$

Answer   9900   (2 marks)

25 Look at the diagram.

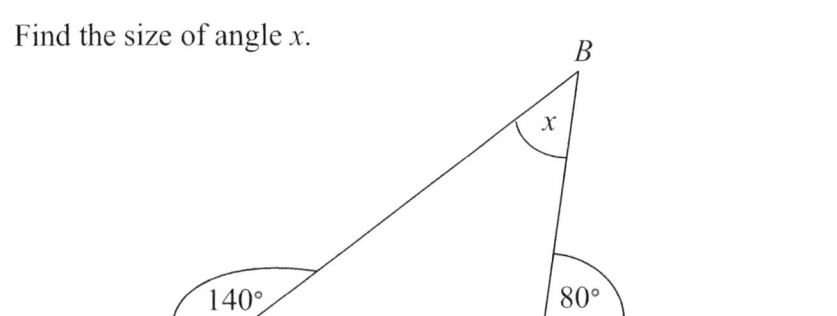

Find the size of angle x.

$\angle BAC = 180° - 140° = 40°$, $\angle ACB = 180° - 80° = 100°$

$x = 180° - \angle BAC - \angle ACB = 180° - 40° - 100° = 40°$

Answer   40°   (2 marks)

26 A is the point $(5,6)$. AB and BC are two sides of a quadrilateral $ABCD$ which has the dotted line as a line of symmetry.

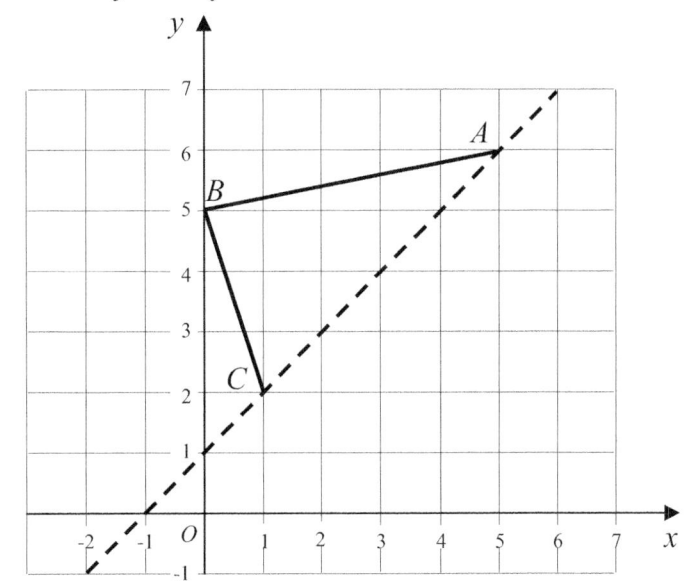

26(a) Write down the coordinates of *B* and *C*.

The coordinates of *B* are (0, 5)

The coordinates of *C* are (1, 2)

Answer   *B*: (0, 5) and *C*: (1, 2)   (2 marks)

26(b) On the diagram, draw the sides *CD* and *AD* of the quadrilateral, and write down the coordinates of *D*.

The point *B* is reflected in the dotted line to get the point *D*(4,1), as shown.

The sides *CD* and *AD* are drawn as shown on the graph.

Answer   (4,1)   (2 marks)

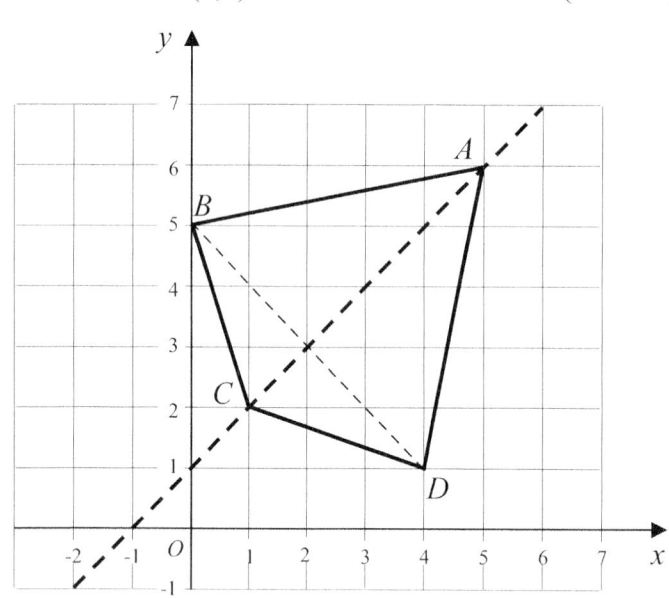

26(c) Write down the name of the quadrilateral *ABCD*.

Answer   Kite   (2 marks)

27 The diagram below is made from three squares.

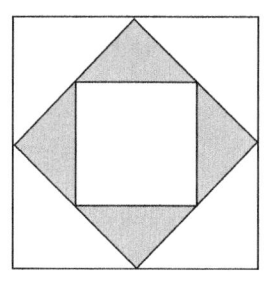

Work out the fraction of the larger square that is shaded.

Give your answer in the simplest form.

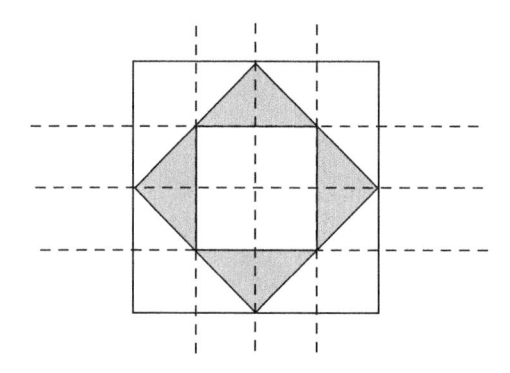

Draw the dotted lines to divide the largest square into 16 portions. The shaded contains 4 portions.

$\dfrac{4}{16} = \dfrac{1}{4}$

Answer $\dfrac{1}{4}$ (3 marks)

28 It takes a team of four people six hours to paint my fence.

28(a) How long would a team of eight people have taken?

$\dfrac{6}{2} = 3$

Answer   3 hours   (2 marks)

5

28(b) One of my neighbours has a similar fence which is twice as long as mine.

She would like the work to be completed in less than five hours.

What is the minimum number of people that she should employ?

Four people would take 12 hours to paint the fence. It would take 48 hours ($4 \times 12\,\text{hr} = 48\,\text{hr}$) for one people to paint the fence.

$$\frac{48}{5} = 9.6$$

Thus the minimum number of people that she should employ is 10 people.

    Answer   10   (3 marks)

29   The diagram shows a circle with a diameter, *AB*. The point *A* has coordinates (4, 3).

The centre has coordinates (8, 7).

Work out the coordinates of the point at the other end of the diameter, *B*.

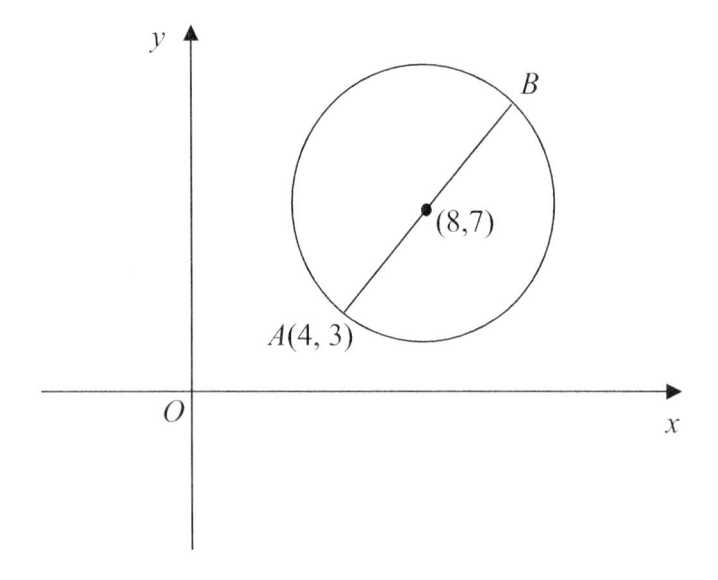

$B_x = A_x + 2(8 - A_x) = 4 + 2(8-4) = 12$

$B_y = A_y + 2(7 - A_y) = 3 + 2(7-3) = 11$

Thus the coordinates of the point, *B*, are (12, 11).

    Answer   (12, 11)   (2 marks)

30(a) Write the correct number in each box.

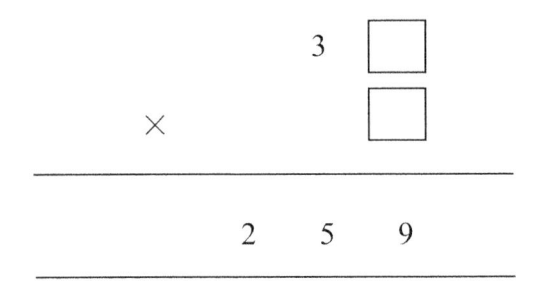

```
        3  □
    ×      □
    ─────────
        2 5 9
    ─────────
```

The numbers are written in the boxes as follows.

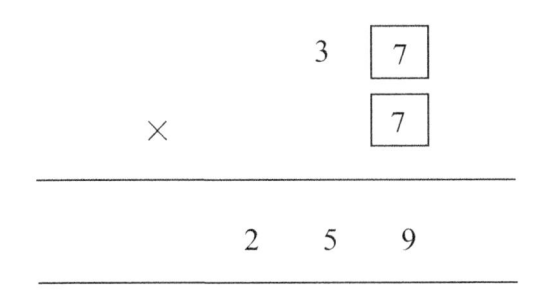

```
        3  7
    ×      7
    ─────────
        2 5 9
    ─────────
```

(2 marks)

30(b) Can you find numbers to replace A, B and C in this sum?

(A, B and C are all different numbers)

```
      A B C
      A B C
    + A B C
    ───────
      B B B
```

```
      1 4 8
      1 4 8
    + 1 4 8
    ───────
      4 4 4
```

Answer   A = 1; B = 4; C = 8   (3 marks)

Paper 6 solutions

1 Circle the highest number in each group.

1(a)   0.609   0.069   0.63   0.063

       0.609   0.069   (0.63)   0.063

       Answer   0.63   (2 marks)

1(b)   -7.5   -1   -8   -1.5

       -7.5   (-1)   -8   -1.5

       Answer   -1   (2 marks)

1(c)   0.09 $\frac{39}{100}$ 0.44 $\frac{2}{5}$

       0.09 $\frac{39}{100}$ (0.44) $\frac{2}{5}$

       Answer   0.44   (2 marks)

2 Write down the next two terms in each of the following sequences:

2(a) $\frac{1}{2}, \frac{1}{4}, \frac{1}{8}, \ldots\ldots, \ldots\ldots$

       $\frac{1}{2}, \frac{1}{4}, \frac{1}{8}, \frac{1}{16}, \frac{1}{32}$

       Answer $\frac{1}{16}, \frac{1}{32}$ (2 marks)

2(b)   10.25,   10.50,   10.75, ……, ……,

       10.25,   10.50,   10.75,   11.00,   11.25

       Answer   11.00, 11.25   (2 marks)

3 Write down all the numbers smaller than 100 which are multiples of both 6 and 8.

$6 = 2 \times 3$, $8 = 2 \times 2 \times 2$

∴ The lowest common multiple (LCM) $= 2 \times 2 \times 2 \times 3 = 24$

$2 \times 24 = 48$, $3 \times 24 = 72$, $4 \times 24 = 96$, $5 \times 24 = 120$

The numbers, which are multiples of both 6 and 8, are 24, 48, 72 and 96.

       Answer   24, 48, 72 and 96   (2 marks)

4   Find the highest common factor (HCF) of 15, 30 and 45

$15 = 3 \times 5$, $30 = 2 \times 3 \times 5$, $45 = 3 \times 3 \times 5$

∴ HCF $= 3 \times 5 = 15$

Answer   15   (2 marks)

5   One third of the pupils in a class are girls. The rest are boys. What is the ratio of girls to boys?

Circle your answer.

1:1   1:2   1:3   1:4   1:5

$\frac{1}{3}$ of the pupils are girls, $\frac{2}{3}$ of the pupils are boys.

$\frac{1}{3} : \frac{2}{3} = 1:2$

1:1   (1:2)   1:3   1:4   1:5

Answer   1:2   (2 marks)

6   Arrange the following fractions in numerical size order, starting with the smallest order.

$\frac{4}{7}$ $\frac{1}{5}$ $\frac{3}{8}$ $\frac{1}{6}$ $\frac{1}{10}$

$\frac{1}{10} = 0.1$, $0.1 < \frac{1}{6} < 0.2$, $\frac{1}{5} = 0.2$, $0.2 < \frac{3}{8} < 0.5$, $\frac{4}{7} > 0.5$

The numerical size order starting from the smallest one is

$\frac{1}{10}$ $\frac{1}{6}$ $\frac{1}{5}$ $\frac{3}{8}$ $\frac{4}{7}$

(2 marks)

7   Write each percentage as a fraction in its simplest form:

7(a)   30%

$30\% = \frac{30}{100} = \frac{3}{10}$

Answer $\frac{3}{10}$ (2 marks)

7(b)   5%

$$5\% = \frac{5}{100} = \frac{1}{20}$$

Answer $\frac{1}{20}$ (2 marks)

7(c) $66\frac{2}{3}\%$

$$66\frac{2}{3}\% = \frac{200}{3}\% = \frac{200}{300} = \frac{2}{3}$$

Answer $\frac{2}{3}$ (2 marks)

7(d)   120%

$$120\% = \frac{120}{100} = \frac{6}{5}$$

Answer $\frac{6}{5}$ (2 marks)

8   This is Jack's function machine.

? → [Subtract 10] → [Divide by 9] → 8

What number did he start with?

$8 \times 9 + 10 = 82$

Thus Jack started with 82.

Answer   82   (2 marks)

9   Round each of the following numbers to the accuracy given in brackets.

9(a)   18.52 (nearest whole number)

Answer   19   (2 marks)

9(b)   120550 (nearest thousand)

Answer   121000   (2 marks)

12

9(c) 26.45789 (nearest tenth)

   Answer   26.5   (2 marks)

10 In the square below, every row, column and diagonal adds up to 30.

Fill the remaining squares with numbers obeying this rule.

12		
	10	
16		

The remaining squares were filled by the numbers as follows.

12	14	4
2	10	18
16	6	8

(2 marks)

11 Jack thinks of a whole number, rounds it to the nearest 100 and gets an answer of 500.

11(a) What is the smallest number that Jack might have thought of?

   Answer   450   (2 marks)

11(b) What is the largest number that Jack might have thought of?

   Answer   549   (2 marks)

12 A clothes shop has a sale. In the sale, normal prices are reduced by 10%.

12(a) The normal price of a tie is £9.00.

Work out the sale price of the tie.

$9 \times (1 - 10\%) = 8.10$

   Answer   £8.10   (2 marks)

10

12(b) The price of a jacket is reduced by £12.00 in the sale.

Work out the normal price of the jacket.

$$\frac{£12.00}{10\%} = £120.00$$

Answer   £120.00   (2 marks)

13 Mr and Mrs Smith take their 3 children to a cinema to watch a film. Tickets cost £8.00 each for adults. The price of a child's ticket is half that of an adult's.

How much does it cost the family to watch the film in the cinema?

$2 \times 8 + 3 \times 4 = 28$

Answer   £28.00   (2 marks)

14 This shape has been created using two identical isosceles triangles ABC and CDE.

$\angle A = \angle E = 30°$

Work out the value of $\angle ACE$

$\angle B = \angle ACB = \angle ECD = \angle D = \frac{180° - 30°}{2} = 75°$

$\angle ACE = 180° - 75° \times 2 = 30°$

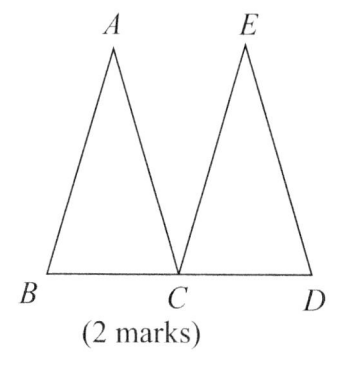

Answer   30°   (2 marks)

15 Here is an L-shape. All lengths are in centimetres.

Work out the area of the shape.

$11 \times 11 - 5 \times (11 - 5) = 121 - 30 = 91$

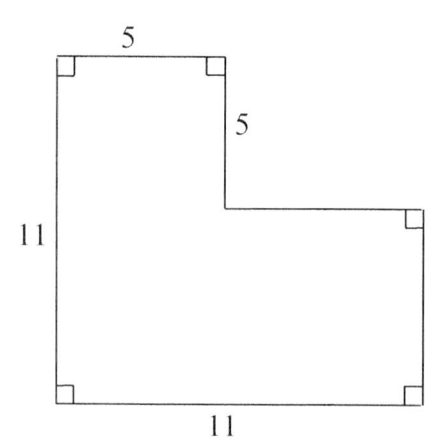

Answer   91 cm²   (2 marks)

8

16 Shape A and shape B are each made from nine identical squares. The perimeter of shape A is 72cm. Work out the perimeter of shape B.

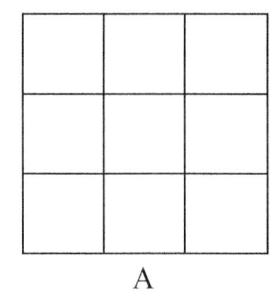

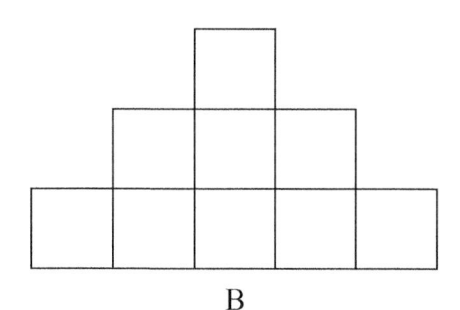

A

B

The length of a side of the square can be calculated as follows:

$\frac{72\,cm}{12} = 6\,cm$, as the perimeter of shape A is 72cm.

The perimeter of shape B is $16 \times 6\,cm = 96\,cm$, as it consists of 16 sides of a square.

Answer   96 cm   (3 marks)

17 The pie chart shows the proportions of different drinks chosen from a machine in one day. There were 15 cartons of orange juice taken. How many cartons of pineapple juice were taken?

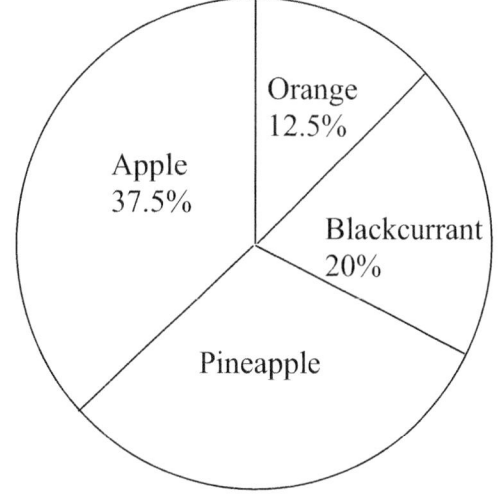

The proportion of pineapple juice is $1 - (37.5\% + 12.5\% + 20\%) = 30\%$

$\frac{30\%}{12.5\%} = 2.4$, it means that the number of the cartons of pineapple juice is 2.4 times the cartons of the orange juice.

$2.4 \times 15 = 36$

Answer   36   (3 marks)

18   *ABCD* is a kite.

Write down the coordinates of vertex *D*.

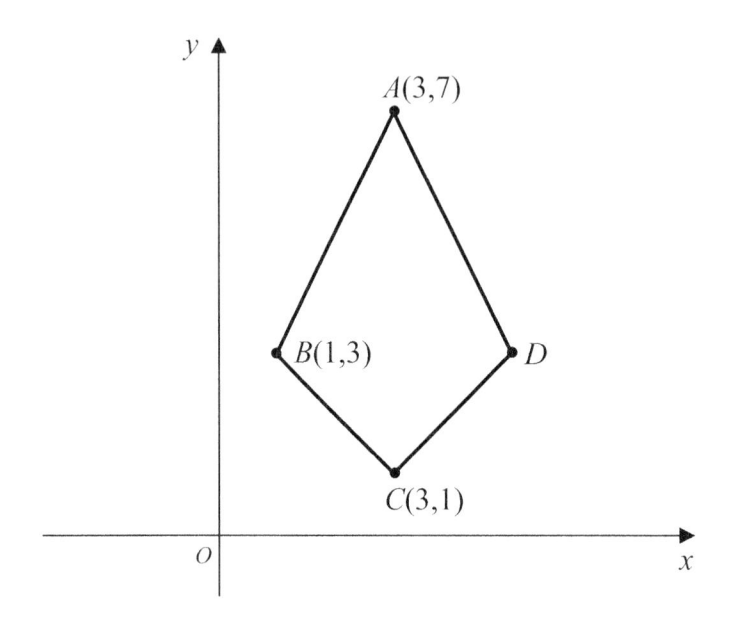

$D_x = B_x + 2(C_x - B_x) = 1 + 2(3-1) = 5$

$D_y = B_y = 3$

Answer   (5, 3)   (3 marks)

19   On Christmas Eve, the temperature in Beijing was $-14°$C.

At the same time, the temperature in Sydney was $18°$C.

19(a)   How many degrees hotter was it in Sydney than in Beijing?

18°C - (-14°C) = 32°C

Answer   32°C   (2 marks)

19(b)   By Christmas Day, the temperature in Beijing had risen by $5°$C.

What was the temperature in Beijing on Christmas Day?

-14°C + 5°C = −9°C

Answer   −9°C   (2 marks)

7

20 The diagram below shows a shaded parallelogram drawn inside a rectangle.

Work out the area of the shaded parallelogram

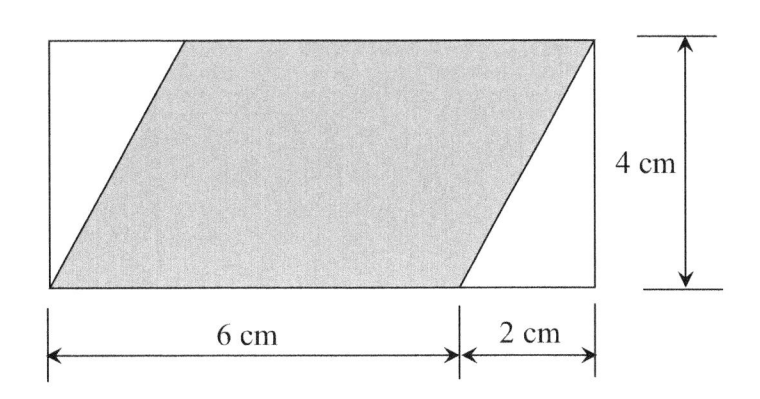

$(6+2) \times 4 - 2 \times \dfrac{2 \times 4}{2} = 32 - 8 = 24$

Answer   24 cm²   (3 marks)

21 Emma shares a large packet of sweets evenly to her 12 friends and then eats the left over sweets. There were 150 sweets in the packet, how many does Emma eat?

$\dfrac{150}{12} = 12 \text{ R } 6$

Answer   6   (2 marks)

22 A rectangle has perimeter 32cm. The length of the rectangle is three times its width. What is the area of the rectangle?

width + length = 16 cm.

width is $\dfrac{1}{4} \times 16 \, cm = 4 \, cm$

length is $\dfrac{3}{4} \times 16 \, cm = 12 \, cm$

The area of the rectangle is $4 \, cm \times 12 \, cm = 48 \, cm^2$

Answer   48 cm²   (2 marks)

23   A pattern is made from two identical squares.

The sides of the squares are parallel to the axes.

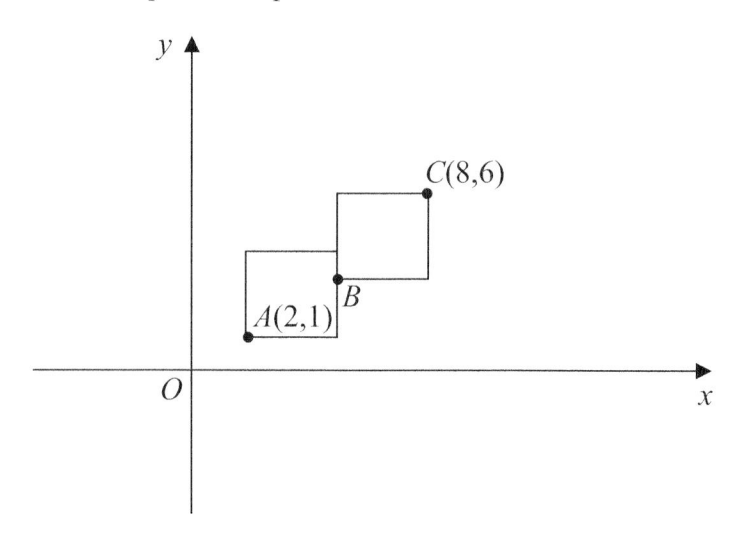

Point A has coordinates (2, 1)

Point C has coordinates (8, 6)

Point B is marked on the diagram.

Work out the coordinates of B.

The length of a side of the square = $\dfrac{C_x - A_x}{2} = \dfrac{8-2}{2} = 3$

$B_x = A_x +$ (the length of a side of the square) $= 2 + 3 = 5$

$B_y = C_y -$ (the length of a side of the square) $= 6 - 3 = 3$

The coordinates of B are (5,3).

Answer   (5,3)   (4 marks)

24(a) On the diagram, draw the image of Shape A when it is reflected in the x-axis.

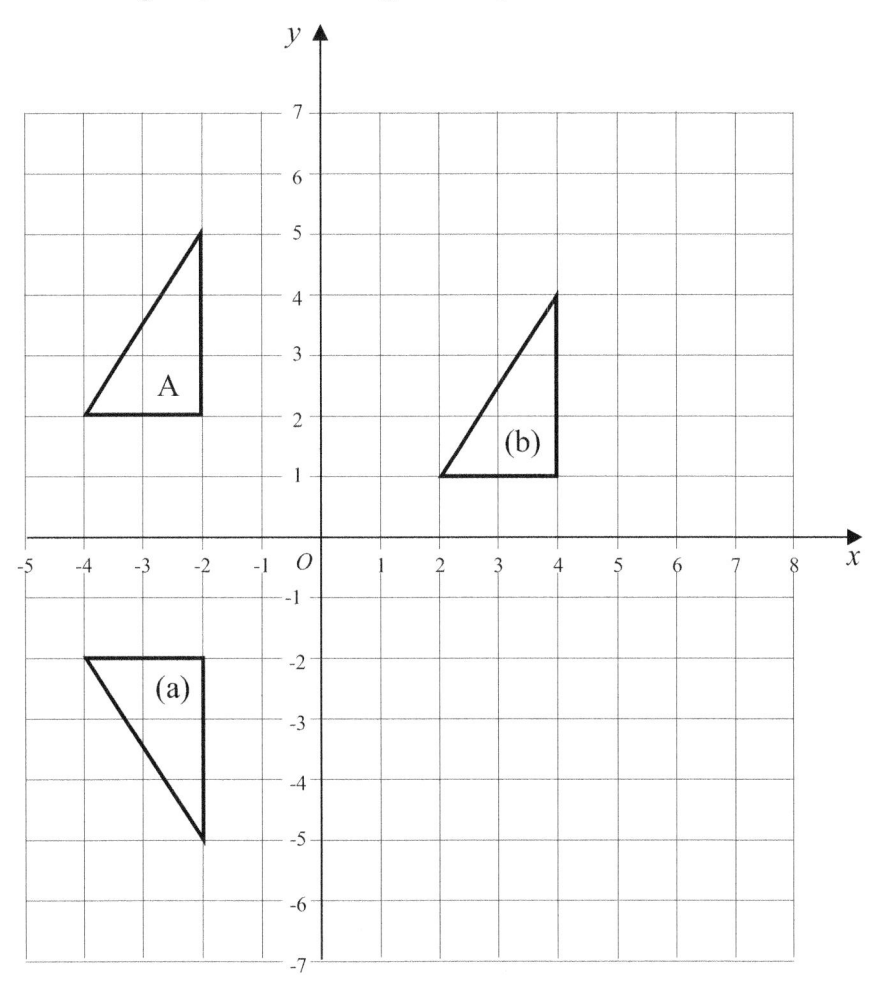

As shown on the diagram. (2 marks)

24(b) On the diagram, draw the image of Shape A again when it is translated by 6 right and 1 down

As shown on the diagram. (2 marks)

25 Emma is choosing pairs of numbers from this list.

　　　4　　23　　45　　58　　120

25(a) She multiplies two numbers together.

Which two numbers should she choose to get an answer between 200 and 300?

$4 \times 58 = 232$

　　　Answer　　　4, 58　　　　　　　　　　(2 marks)

25(b) Which two numbers have the highest common factor (HCF)?

$4 = 2 \times 2$, $23 = 1 \times 23$, $45 = 3 \times 3 \times 5$, $58 = 2 \times 29$, $120 = 2 \times 2 \times 2 \times 3 \times 5$

45 and 120 give the highest common factor 15:　$3 \times 5 = 15$

　　　Answer　　　45, 120　　　　　　　　(3 marks)

26 The table shows Ann's marks in two tests.

Test	Mark
1	60 out of 80
2	70 out of 100

In which test did Ann do better?

You **must** show your working.

$\frac{60}{80} = 75\%$, $\frac{70}{100} = 70\%$

∴ Ann did better in Test 1.

　　　Answer　　　Test 1　　　　　　　　(3 marks)

27 Jack is 30 years older than Mark. In 18 years Jack will be twice Mark's age. How old is Mark?

If the Mark's age is x years old, in 18 years, Mark will be $(x+18)$ years old, Jack will be $(x+18+30)$ years old.

$(x+18+30) = 2(x+18) \Rightarrow x = 12$

　　　Answer　　　12 years old　　　　　　(3 marks)

28 The sum of five consecutive whole numbers is 75.

What is the smallest of these five numbers?

The third number is: $\frac{75}{5} = 25$

∴ The smallest of these five numbers is: $25 - 2 = 23$

Answer   23   (3 marks)

29 I flip a fair coin that has the number 3 on one side and the number 7 on the other side. At the same time I roll a fair six sided die that has the numbers 1 to 6 on it. Then I add the two numbers. If I do this 60 times how many times would you expect me to get a total of 7?

The probability for the flipping coin to land with the number 3 on it is $\frac{1}{2}$.

The probability for the rolling a fair six sided die with the number 4 on it is $\frac{1}{6}$.

The probability for the flipping the coin and rolling die each once to get the total of the number 7 is $\frac{1}{2} \times \frac{1}{6} = \frac{1}{12}$.

If I do this 60 times, $60 \times \frac{1}{12} = 5$, you would expect me 5 times to get a total of 7.

Answer   5   (3 marks)

30(a) In this multiplication, each letter stands for a different digit. What digit does C represent? Show your working.

```
  A 6 B 4
×       7
---------
  C 6 D 9 8
```

$$\begin{array}{r} \overset{4}{}\overset{2}{} \\ 6\;6\;1\;4 \\ \times 7 \\ \hline 4\;6\;2\;9\;8 \end{array}$$

Answer   4   (2 marks)

30(b) A, B and C are all different numbers.

Can you find numbers to replace A, B and C in this sum?

```
         A              6
         A              6
+     B  B       +   9  9
———————————      ———————————
      C  C  C        1  1  1
———————————      ———————————
                    2
```

Answer   A = 6; B = 9; C = 1   (3 marks)

Paper 7 solutions

1 Work out the missing values

1(a) 11% of 3600 = …………

11% of 3600 = 396

Answer   396   (2 marks)

1(b) ……… % of 52 = 13

$\frac{13}{52} = 0.25 = 25\% \Rightarrow 25\% \times 52 = 13$

Answer   25   (2 marks)

1(c) 15 % of …………. = 60

$\frac{60}{15\%} = 400 \Rightarrow 15\% \times 400 = 60$

Answer   400   (2 marks)

2(a) Calculate 50% of 20% of 5000

$50\% \times 20\% \times 5000 = 0.1 \times 5000 = 500$

Answer   500   (2 marks)

2(b) Calculate 20192019 ÷ 2019

```
         10001
2019 / 20192019
       2019
       ────
         2019
         2019
         ────
            0
```

20192019 ÷ 2019 = 10001

Answer   10001   (2 marks)

3 Emma correctly worked out that 2451 ÷ 43 = 57.

3(a) What is the value of 43 × 57 + 9 ?

$43 \times 57 + 9 = 2451 + 9 = 2460$

Answer   2460   (2 marks)

12

85

3(b) What is the value of 2.451 ÷ 0.43?

$$2.451 \div 0.43 = \frac{2451}{1000} \div \frac{43}{100} = \frac{2451}{43} \div \frac{1000}{100} = 57 \div 10 = 5.7$$

Answer 5.7   (2 marks)

4 The ratio of flour to sugar in a cake is 11 : 4.

If 200 grams of sugar was used to make the cake, how much flour was used?

$$200 \times \frac{11}{4} = 550$$

Answer 550 grams   (2 marks)

5 Write these decimals in order of size, starting with the smallest:

2.3 2.23 2.303 2.203

Answer 2.203 2.23 2.3 2.303 (2 marks)

6 Emma buys a pair of jeans.

20% VAT is added to the price of the jeans.

Emma has to pay a total of £60.

What is the price of the jeans with **no** VAT added?

$$\frac{60}{1+20\%} = 50$$

Answer £50   (2 marks)

7 The students on a Geography trip to Iceland arrive at Heathrow Airport at 10:45.

Their flight leaves at 13:05.

How many minutes do they have to wait at the airport before their flight leaves?

13 h 5 min − 10 h 45 min = 12 h 65 min − 10 h 45 min = 2 h 20 min = 140 min

Answer 140 minutes   (2 marks)

8   The table shows the technology subjects studies by a group of students.

	Art	Design Tech	Textiles	Total
Boys	23		0	60
Girls		14	6	
Total	53		6	

Complete the table above.

The completed the table as follows.

	Art	Design Tech	Textiles	Total
Boys	23	37	0	60
Girls	30	14	6	50
Total	53	51	6	110

(3 marks)

9   Jack paid a £50 deposit for a TV, then monthly payments of £25 each. The TV cost £550.

How many monthly payments did Jack have to make to buy it?

$$\frac{550-50}{25} = 20$$

Answer   20   (2 marks)

10 There are 600 pupils at Jack's school. There are 50 more girls than boys.

How many girls are there?

$$\frac{600}{2} + 25 = 325$$

Answer   325   (2 marks)

7

87

11 MAGNUM washing-up liquid is sold in two quantities, 500 ml and 250 ml. They cost £1.05 and 60 p respectively.

Which of these two quantities is the better value for money?

500 ml: $\dfrac{£1.05}{500\,\text{ml}} = 0.21\text{p/ml}$

250 ml: $\dfrac{60\text{p}}{250\,\text{ml}} = 0.24\text{p/ml}$

∴ 500 ml is the better value for money.

Answer   500 ml   (2 marks)

12 Match the following numbers to the labelled points on the number line.

1·796   1·799   1·776   1·792   1·814   1·782

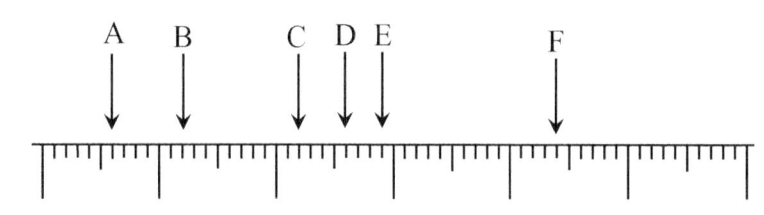

12(a) 1·796 is matched with .... (2 marks)

1·796 is matched with D

12(b) 1·799 is matched with .... (2 marks)

1·799 is matched with E

12(c) 1·776 is matched with .... (2 marks)

1·776 is matched with A

12(d) 1·792 is matched with .... (2 marks)

1·792 is matched with C

12(e) 1·814 is matched with .... (2 marks)

1·814 is matched with F

12(f) 1·782 is matched with ………………………… (2 marks)

1·782 is matched with B

13 The difference between $\frac{1}{4}$ of a number and $\frac{1}{5}$ of the same number is 5.

What is the number?

$$\frac{5}{\frac{1}{4}-\frac{1}{5}} = \frac{5}{\frac{5}{20}-\frac{4}{20}} = \frac{5}{\frac{1}{20}} = 5 \times 20 = 100$$

Answer   100   (2 marks)

14 Kate takes one a day of each of two types of tablet. One type of tablet is in packets of 15 and the other type is in packets of 20. She starts new packets of both on 1st March.

On what date will she next start new packets of both?

The lowest common multiple (LCM) of 15 and 20 can be calculate as follows:

$15 = 3 \times 5$, $20 = 2 \times 2 \times 5$

LCM $= 2 \times 2 \times 3 \times 5 = 60$

There are 31 days in March, 30 days in April and 31 days in May.

She will next start new packets of both on the 30th May.

Answer   On the 30th May   (3 marks)

15 Anna decides to share her pizza with two of her friends. She gives one friend a fifth of the pizza and the other friend three tenths of the pizza.

What fraction of the pizza is left for Anna?

$$1 - \frac{1}{5} - \frac{3}{10} = 1 - \frac{5}{10} = \frac{1}{2}$$

Answer $\frac{1}{2}$ (2 marks)

16   Mr Fryer and his sons Jack and Mark have the same birthday. Today, Mr Fryer is 38, Jack is 10 and Mark is 7.

How old will they be when Mr Fryer's age is the sum of his sons' ages?

Mr Fryer ……………..years

Jack ……………..years

Mark ……………..years

In x years, Mr Fryer's age will be the sum of his sons' ages.

In x years, the sum of his sons' ages will be: $x+10+x+7=2x+17$

Mr Fryer's age will be: $x+38$

$x+38=2x+17 \Rightarrow x=21$

In 21 years,

$38+21=59$, $10+21=31$, $7+21=28$

Mr Fryer will be 59 years old

Jack will be 31 years old

Mark will be 28 years old

(3 marks)

17   Three boxes (A, B and C) contain red balls or yellow balls or both.

Each box contains the same number of balls.

Box A contains all twelve of the red balls and one ninth of the yellow balls.

17(a) How many yellow balls are there altogether?

Box A contains all twelve of the red balls and one ninth of the yellow balls, it means that $\frac{8}{9}$ of the yellow balls are in the other two boxes, and each box contains $\frac{4}{9}$ of the yellow balls.

If the number of yellow balls is x, then $12+\frac{1}{9}x=\frac{4}{9}x \Rightarrow x=36$

Answer   36   (2 marks)

17(b) How many balls are there in each box?

$\frac{4}{9} \times 36 = 16$

Answer   16   (2 marks)

7

18 Emma has 6 equilateral triangles, each with a perimeter of 15 cm. She fits them together to make a regular hexagon.

Work out the perimeter of the hexagon.

Note: Sketching the diagram may help you work out much easier.

The regular hexagon is sketched as shown.

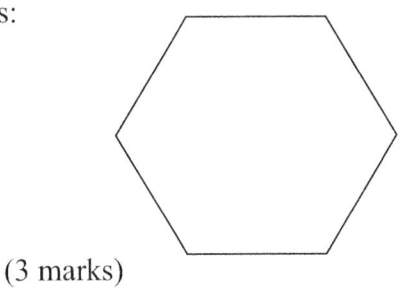

The length of a side of the each equilateral triangle is:

$$\frac{15\,cm}{3} = 5\,cm$$

The perimeter of the hexagon is:

$5\,cm \times 6 = 30\,cm$

Answer   30 cm   (3 marks)

19 Jack has 4 equilateral triangles, each with a perimeter of 15 cm. He fits them together to make a larger equilateral triangle.

Work out the perimeter of the larger equilateral triangle.

Note: Sketching the diagram may help you work out much easier.

The larger equilateral triangle is sketched as shown.

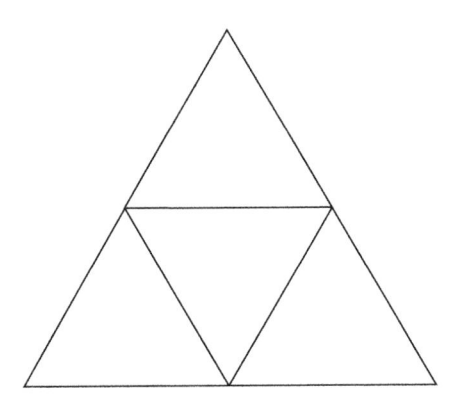

The length of a side of the each equilateral triangle is:

$$\frac{15\,cm}{3} = 5\,cm$$

The perimeter of the larger equilateral triangle is:

$5\,cm \times 6 = 30\,cm$

Answer   30 cm   (3 marks)

20 Here are triangles.

Work out the values of *a* and *b*.

In triangle *ABC*

$2a + \angle ACB = 180°$

$b + \angle ACB = 180°$

$\therefore b = 2a$

$a + b + b = 180° \Rightarrow a + 2a + 2a = 180° \Rightarrow a = 36°$, $b = 2a = 72°$

Answer $a = 36°$, $b = 72°$ (2 marks)

21 40 people were asked to choose a drink.

One quarter chose tea. Three eighths of them chose coffee. 30% of them chose orange juice. The rest chose water.

21(a) How many people chose water?

$40 - \dfrac{40}{4} - \dfrac{3}{8} \times 40 - 30\% \times 40 = 40 - 10 - 15 - 12 = 3$

Answer   3   (2 marks)

21(b) Emma drew a pie chart to show all their choices.

How many degrees should 'Water' have on her pie chart?

$\dfrac{3}{40} \times 360° = 27°$

Answer   27°   (2 marks)

22 Here are four cards.

| 1 | 5 | 3 | 4 |

22(a) Choose two cards to make a two-digit multiple of 6.

$54 = 6 \times 9$

Answer   Cards with numbers 4 and 5

(2 marks)

8

22(b)　Choose two cards to make a two-digit factor of 65.

65 = 5 × 13

　　　　Answer　　　Cards with numbers 1 and 3

　　　　　　　　　　　　　　　　(2 marks)

23　Jack picks one of these cards at random.

| 1 | 2 | 3 | 4 | 5 | 6 | 7 | 8 | 9 |

Here are some possible outcomes.

A　　The number on the card will be a factor of 12.

B　　The number on the card will be a multiple of 2.

C　　The number on the card will be a multiple of 3.

D　　The number on the card will be a multiple of 4.

E　　The number on the card will be a square number.

23(a)　Which of these outcomes (A, B, C, D, E) is the most likely to happen?

23(b)　Which of these outcomes (A, B, C, D, E) is the least likely to happen?

23(c)　Which two of these outcomes (A, B, C, D, E) are equally likely to happen?

The numbers, 1, 2, 3, 4 and 6, on the cards, are factors of 12.

The probability for the number on the card, which is a factor of 12, is $\frac{5}{9}$

The numbers, 2, 4, 6 and 8, on the cards, are multiples of 2.

The probability for the number on the card, which is a multiple of 2, is $\frac{4}{9}$

The numbers, 3, 6 and 9, on the cards, are multiples of 3.

The probability for the number on the card, which is a multiple of 3, is $\frac{3}{9} = \frac{1}{3}$

The numbers, 4 and 8, on the card, are multiples of 4.

The probability for the number on the card, which is a multiple of 4, is $\frac{2}{9}$

The numbers, 1, 4 and 9, on the cards, are square numbers.

The probability for the number on the card, which is a square number, is $\frac{3}{9} = \frac{1}{3}$

23(a)　Which of these outcomes (A, B, C, D, E) is the most likely to happen?

　　　　Answer　　　A　　　　　　　　(2 marks)

23(b) Which of these outcomes (A, B, C, D, E) is the least likely to happen?

Answer   D   (2 marks)

23(c) Which two of these outcomes (A, B, C, D, E) are equally likely to happen?

Answer   C and E   (2 marks)

24 In this partly completed pyramid, each rectangle is to be filled with the sum of the numbers in the two triangles just below it.

Which number should replace x?

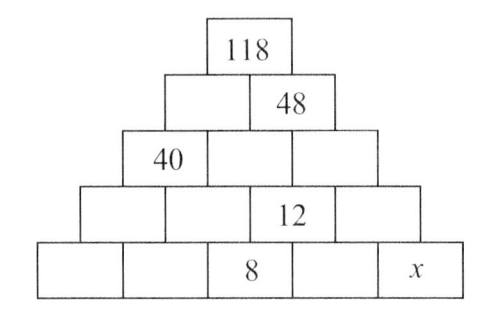

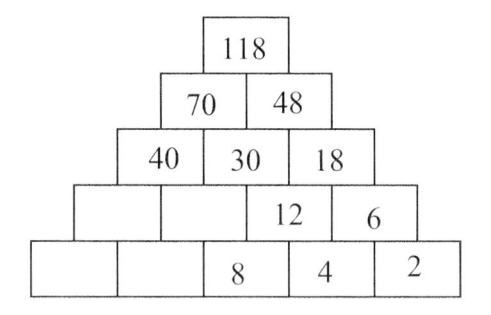

```
        118
      48
    40
         12
       8       x
```

```
        118
       70  48
      40  30  18
           12   6
         8   4   2
```

As shown on the diagram, $x = 2$

Answer   2   (3 marks)

25 Here is a regular octagon.

Shade in $\frac{3}{4}$ of this shape

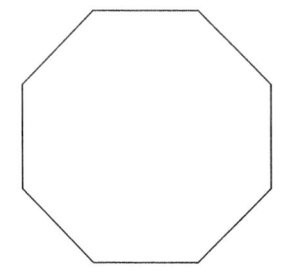

First use the lines to equally divide the regular octagon into 8 triangles, and shade the 6 of 8 triangles, which $\frac{3}{4}$ of this shape is shaded as shown on the diagram.

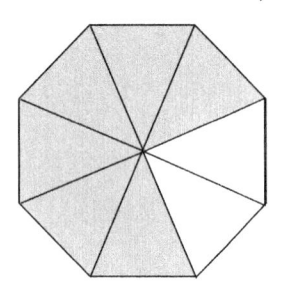

(3 marks)

26 This diagram shows a regular hexagon.

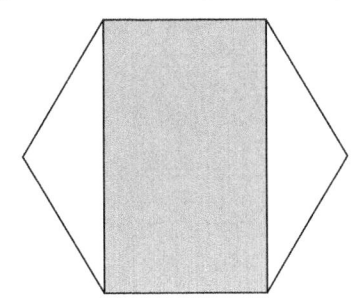

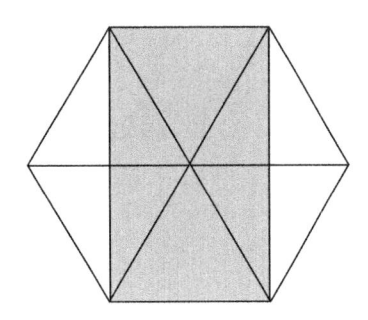

What fraction of the hexagon is shaded?

As it is a regular hexagon, it can be equally divided into 6 triangles by lines.

It is easy to see that the shaded area is equivalent to 4 triangles.

$\frac{4}{6} = \frac{2}{3}$

Answer $\frac{2}{3}$ (3 marks)

27 Work out the number from the following clues:

A   It is a whole number.

B   It is less than 80.

C   It is square number.

D   It is one more than a multiple of 5.

E   3 is a factor of this number.

The numbers, which are square numbers and also less than 80, are

64, 49, 36, 25, 16, 9, 4 and 1.

The numbers, which is one more than a multiple of 5, are 36 and 16.

3 is a factor of 36.

Answer 36 (3 marks)

28 You are told that $121 \times 121 = 14641$

Use this fact and the idea above to work out the value of 119×123. (Note: Do not multiply 119 by 123)

$119 \times 123 = (121-2) \times 123 = 121 \times 123 - 2 \times 123 = 121 \times (121+2) - 2 \times (121+2)$
$= 121 \times 121 + 212 \times 2 - 2 \times 121 - 2 \times 2 = 14641 - 4 = 14637$

Answer 14637 (3 marks)

9

29 Emma spent $\frac{1}{3}$ of her money on a new top and $\frac{1}{3}$ of the remainder on a skirt. She had £8 left. How much did Emma spend altogether?

After she spent $\frac{1}{3}$ of the remainder on a skirt, £8 was left, which is $\frac{2}{3}$ of the remainder. Therefore $\frac{1}{3}$ of the remainder was £4 which she spent on the skirt. The remainder was £12.

After she spent $\frac{1}{3}$ of her money on a new top, she had $\frac{2}{3}$ of her money left, which was the remainder, £12, therefore $\frac{1}{3}$ of her money is £6 which she spent on the new top.

Emma spent £6 on the new top and £4 for on the skirt. Altogether it was £10.

Answer   £10   (3 marks)

Alternative method: Emma had £x.

$x - \frac{1}{3}x - \frac{1}{3}(x - \frac{1}{3}x) = 8 \Rightarrow x = 18$. $\frac{1}{3}x = \frac{1}{3} \times 18 = 6 \Rightarrow$ £6 on the new top.

$\frac{x-6}{3} = \frac{18-6}{3} = 4 \Rightarrow$ £4 on the skirt.

Altogether it was £4 + £6 = £10

30 A cuboid has faces with areas of 40 cm², 55 cm² and 88 cm². What are the lengths of its sides?

$55 = 5 \times 11$, $88 = 8 \times 11$, $40 = 5 \times 8$

The lengths of its sides of the cuboid are 5 cm, 8 cm and 11 cm, respectively.

Answer   5 cm, 8 cm, 11 cm.   (3 marks)

Paper 8 solutions

1   You are told that $12 \times 1284 = 15408$

Use this answer to work out the values of:

1(a) 6×1284

$$6 \times 1284 = \frac{12 \times 1284}{2} = \frac{15408}{2} = 7704$$

         Answer   7704   (2 marks)

1(b) 24×128.4

$$24 \times 128.4 = 2 \times \frac{12 \times 1284}{10} = \frac{2 \times 15408}{10} = \frac{30816}{10} = 3081.6$$

         Answer   3081.6   (2 marks)

2(a) 360×19 is more than 350×19

How much more?

$$360 \times 19 - 350 \times 19 = 10 \times 19 = 190$$

         Answer   190   (2 marks)

2(b)   Work out the product of 499 and 99.

$$499 \times 99 = 499 \times 100 - 499 = 49900 - 499 = 49900 - 500 + 1 = 49400 + 1 = 49401$$

         Answer   49401   (2 marks)

3(a)   Find 15% of 240

$$15\% \times 240 = \frac{\overset{3}{\cancel{15}}}{\underset{20}{\cancel{100}}} \times 240 = \frac{3}{\underset{1}{\cancel{20}}} \times \overset{12}{\cancel{240}} = 3 \times 12 = 36$$

         Answer   36   (2 marks)

3(b)   Find the difference between 10% of £20 and 20% of £10.

$$10\% \times 20 - 20\% \times 10 = 0.1 \times 20 - 0.2 \times 10 = 2 - 2 = 0$$

         Answer   0   (2 marks)

12

3(c) What is five sevenths of 707?

$$\frac{5}{7} \times 707 = 5 \times \frac{707}{7} = 5 \times 101 = 505$$

        Answer   505   (2 marks)

4 Which fraction is half way between $\frac{1}{7}$ and $\frac{1}{3}$

Give your answer in its simplest form.

$$\frac{\frac{1}{7}+\frac{1}{3}}{2} = \frac{\frac{3}{21}+\frac{7}{21}}{2} = \frac{\frac{10}{21}}{2} = \frac{5}{21}$$

        Answer $\frac{5}{21}$ (2 marks)

5 Change 0.36 to a fraction

Give your answer in its simplest form.

$$0.36 = \frac{\cancel{36}^{9}}{\cancel{100}_{25}} = \frac{9}{25}$$

        Answer $\frac{9}{25}$ (2 marks)

6 Two numbers have a sum of 11 and a product of 24. What is their difference?

$24 = 2 \times 12 = 3 \times 8 = 4 \times 6$, $3 + 8 = 11$

∴ Two numbers are 3 and 8.

$8 - 3 = 5$

        Answer   5   (3 marks)

7 Arrange the numbers, 5, 4, 9 and 2 to make the largest possible four-digit number which is a multiple of 5.

        Answer   9425   (3 marks)

12

8   If it is -26.5°C in Canada and 34.5°C in Australia, what is the difference in temperature?

$34.5°C - (-26.5°C) = 34.5°C + 26.5°C = 61°C$

Answer   61°C   (3 marks)

9   Write down (in simplest form) the fraction that the arrow is pointing to.

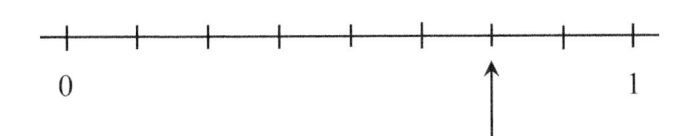

$\frac{6}{8} = \frac{3}{4}$

Answer $\frac{3}{4}$ (3 marks)

10 What is the size of angle "a"?

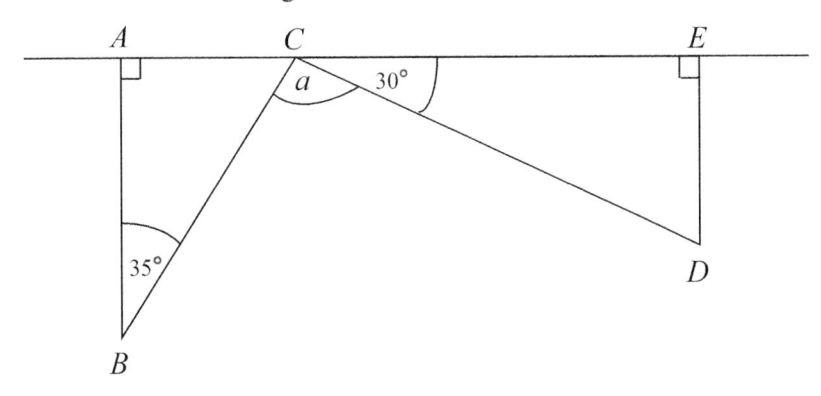

$\angle ACB = 90° - 35°$, $a = 180° - \angle ACB - \angle DCE = 180° - (90° - 35°) - 30° = 95°$

Answer   95°   (3 marks)

11   Here is diagram. $AB = AC$. Work out the values of x and y.

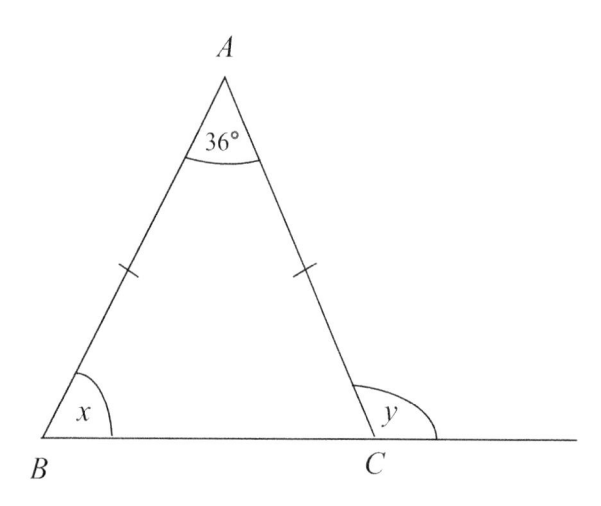

$\angle ACB = \angle B = x = \dfrac{180° - 36°}{2} = 72°$

$y = 180° - \angle ACB = 180° - 72° = 108°$

Answer $x = 72°$, $y = 108°$ (3 marks)

12   Shade 44% of this shape.

$44\% \times 5 \times 5 = \dfrac{44}{100} \times 5 \times 5 = \dfrac{44}{20} \times 5 = \dfrac{44}{4} = 11$

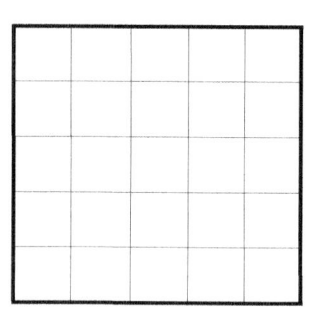

$\dfrac{11}{25}$ of this shape needs to be shaded as follows.

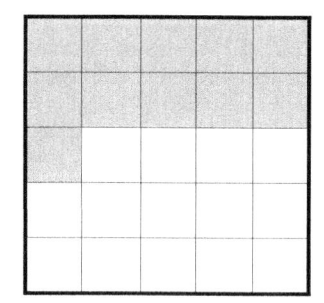

(3 marks)

13 Find the area of the following shaded shapes.

Scale: 1 square = 1 cm²

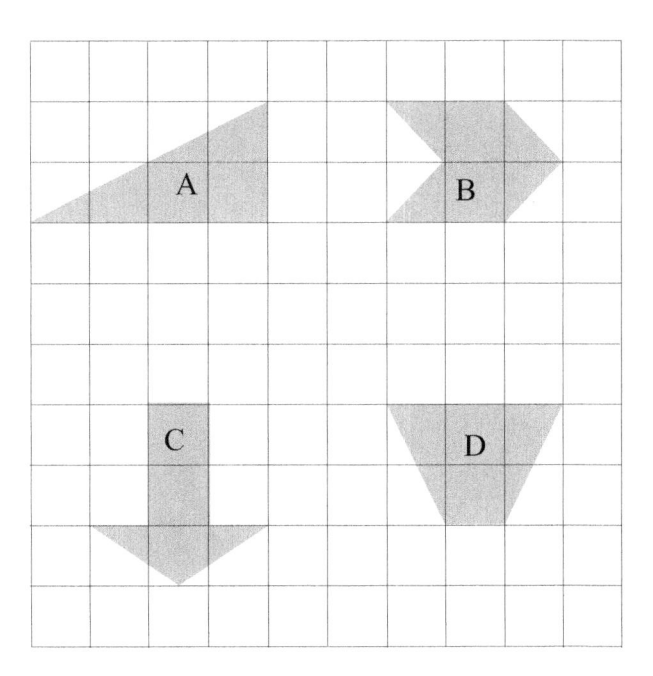

A: $\dfrac{4\,\text{cm} \times 2\,\text{cm}}{2} = 4\,\text{cm}^2$

B: $2 \times 2\,\text{cm} \times 1\,\text{cm} = 4\,\text{cm}^2$

C: $2\,\text{cm} \times 1\,\text{cm} + \dfrac{3\,\text{cm} \times 1\,\text{cm}}{2} = 3.5\,\text{cm}^2$

D: $\dfrac{1\,\text{cm} + 3\,\text{cm}}{2} \times 2\,\text{cm} = 4\,\text{cm}^2$

Answer A: $4\,\text{cm}^2$; B: $4\,\text{cm}^2$; C: $3.5\,\text{cm}^2$; D: $4\,\text{cm}^2$

(4 marks)

14   Here is a straight-line graph.

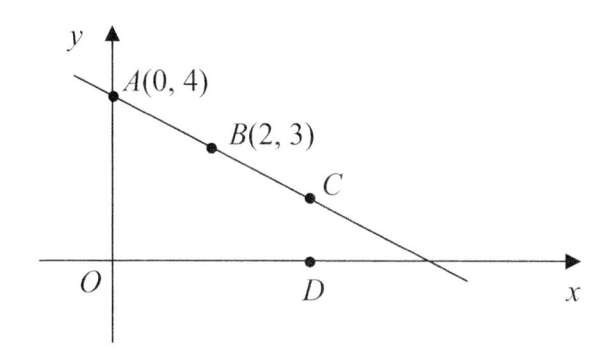

Point B is the midpoint of points A and C.

14(a)   What are the coordinates of point C?

$C_x = 2B_x = 4$

$C_y = B_y - (A_y - B_y) = 3 - (4-3) = 2$

The coordinates of point C are (4, 2).

Answer   (4, 2)   (3 marks)

14(b)   Point D is directly below point C as shown.

What are the coordinates of point D?

$D_x = C_x = 4$, $D_y = 0$

The coordinates of point D are (4, 0).

Answer   (4, 0)   (3 marks)

15   I want to cut out a circle of radius 5.5 cm from a square piece of card.

What is the area of the smallest square I can use?

The length of a side of the smallest square is $2 \times 5.5 \, \text{cm} = 11 \, \text{cm}$

The area of the smallest square is $(11 \, \text{cm})^2 = 121 \, \text{cm}^2$

Answer $121 \, \text{cm}^2$ (3 marks)

16   Four bells ring at intervals of 2, 6, 9 and 12 seconds.

If they are all rung at the same time, how many seconds will pass before they all ring at the same time again?

$6 = 2 \times 3, \ 9 = 3 \times 3, \ 12 = 2 \times 2 \times 3$

The lowest common multiple (LCM) of 2, 6, 9 and 12 can be calculated as follows:

LCM $= 2 \times 2 \times 3 \times 3 = 36$

∴ 36 seconds will pass before they all ring at the same time again.

Answer   36 seconds   (3 marks)

17   When my age is divided by 2, 3, 4 or 6, there is always a remainder of 1. But when divided by 5 there is no remainder. I am less than 50 years old.

How old am I?

The multiples of 5 are, 5, 10, 15, 20, 25, 30, 35, 40 and 45.

When my age is divided by 2, there is always a remainder of 1. It means my age is odd number; it could be 5, 15, 25, 35 or 45.

Only the number, 25, has a remainder of 1 if it is divided by 2, 3, 4 or 6.

Answer   25 years old   (3 marks)

18   I opened a book at random and multiplied the two page numbers together.

The answer was 156. What were the numbers on the two pages?

$156 = 2 \times 78 = 4 \times 39 = 4 \times 3 \times 13 = 12 \times 13$

∴ The numbers, 12 and 13, were on the two pages.

Answer   12, 13   (3 marks)

19   Bill, Mark, Jack, Alex and Emma went to the cinema. They spent £30 on tickets and £20·50 on food. They shared the cost equally.

How much did each have to pay?

$\dfrac{30 + 20.50}{5} = 10.10$

Answer   £10.10   (3 marks)

20 A street has forty six houses, door plate numbers are from 1 to 46.

How many digit 2s are used on the complete set of door plates for this street?

The numbers from 1 to 10, there is one digit 2.

The numbers from 11 to 20, there are two digit 2s.

The numbers from 21 to 30, there are ten digit 2s.

The numbers from 31 to 40, there is one digit 2.

The numbers from 41 to 46, there is one digit 2.

The total number of the digit 2s are $1+2+10+1+1=15$.

  Answer 15 (3 marks)

21 In Beijing China the time is 8 hours ahead of the UK. Emma decides to phone her Great Aunt Maria at 23:00 UK time on the 30th January.

What is the time and date in Beijing when Maria receives the call?

  Answer Time: 7:00; Date: 31st January

  (3 marks)

22   Of the 30 boys in a class, 28 are right-handed. If 10 of the boys in the class wear glasses.

What is the minimum number of boys in the class who are both right-handed and wear glasses?

Draw a table by the known information about the 30 boys below.

	Right-handed	Left-handed	Total
Wear glasses			10
Not wear glasses			
Total	28		30

$30 - 28 = 2 \Rightarrow$ 2 boys are left-handed, fill "2" for "left-handed" in the table.

The maximum number of boys who are both left-handed and wear glasses, is 2, fill "2" for "both left-handed and wear glasses" in the table.

$10 - 2 = 8 \Rightarrow$ The minmum number of the boys is 8 who are both right-handed and wear glasses, fill "8" for are "both right-handed and wear glasses" in the table.

In the similar way, remaining numbers can be filled in the table as follows.

	Right-handed	Left-handed	Total
Wear glasses	8	2	10
Not wear glasses	20	0	20
Total	28	2	30

Answer   8   (3 marks)

23   Emma, Jack and Mark share some money. Emma gets £10 more than Jack, Jack gets £15 more than Mark. The total amount of the money is £100.

How much does Mark get?

If Mark gets £x, $x + (x+15) + (x+10+15) = 100 \Rightarrow 3x + 40 = 100 \Rightarrow x = 20$

Answer   £20   (3 marks)

24   What is the angle between the hands of a clock at half past ten?

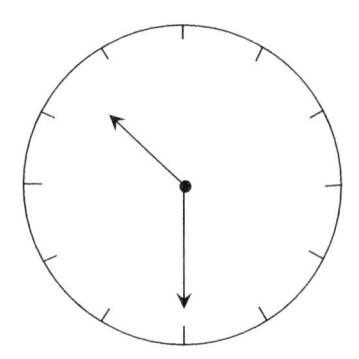

$\dfrac{360°}{12} \times 4.5 = 30° \times 4.5 = 135°$

   Answer   135°   (3 marks)

25   On the 1st January 2016 my grandmother was 80 years old. Her daughter was 40 years old on the 1st January 2004. How old was my grandmother when her daughter was born?

From 2004 to 2016, it passed 12 years, as $2016 - 2004 = 12$.

On the 1st January 2004, my grandmother was 68 years old, as $80 - 12 = 68$. My grandmother is older than her daughter 28 years old, as $68 - 40 = 28$, therefore my grandmother was 28 years old when her daughter was born.

   Answer   28 years old   (3 marks)

26   Jack's bucket weighs 20 kg when full of water. After he pours half the water from the bucket, it weighs 13 kg.

What is the weight of the empty bucket?

The weight of the half of the water is $(20-13)\,\text{kg} = 7\,\text{kg}$. The weight of all of the water is $2 \times 7\,\text{kg} = 14\,\text{kg}$.

The weight of the empty bucket is $(20-14)\,\text{kg} = 6\,\text{kg}$

   Answer   6 kg   (3 marks)

27 In a barn there are only horses and hens. If they have 60 heads and 140 legs in total, how many horses and how many hens are there?

If the number of hens is x, the number of horses is $60-x$, the number of legs for hens is $2x$, the number of legs for horses is $4(60-x)$

$2x + 4(60-x) = 140 \Rightarrow 240 - 2x = 140 \Rightarrow x = 50$, $60 - x = 10$

∴ The number of hens is 50, the number of horses is 10.

Answer   the number of hens: 50; the number of horses: 10

(3 marks)

28 A number of children are standing in a circle. They are evenly spaced and the 6th child is directly opposite the 17th child. How many children are there altogether?

On the left side from the 6th to the 17th, there are 10 children (= 17-6-1), excluding the 6th child and 17th child. Therefore there are 10 children on the right side.

Including the 6th child and 17th child, the number of children is:

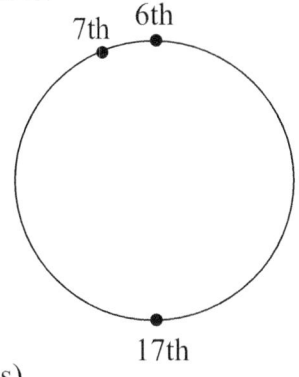

$2 \times 10 + 2 = 22$

Answer   22   (3 marks)

29 Jack and Mark are having a race. Jack starts running from the start line at 10m/s. Three seconds later Mark starts running from the start line at 12m/s.

29(a) How long after Jack starts running does Mark catch up with him?

If Mark catches up with Jack after Jack starts running x seconds, then

$x \times 10 = (x-3) \times 12 \Rightarrow 10x = 12x - 36 \Rightarrow x = 18$

Answer   18 seconds   (3 marks)

29(b) How far are they both from the start line when Mark catches up with Jack?

$18 \times 10 = 180$

Answer   180 m   (2 marks)

11

30 Write the correct digit in each box.

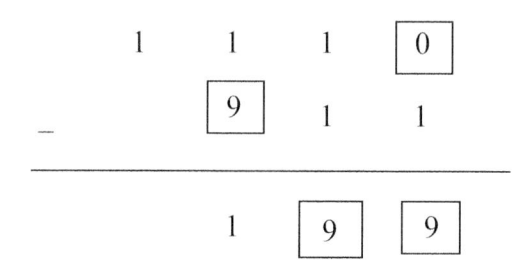

30(a)

```
    1  1  1  □
 −     □  1  1
 ─────────────
       1  □  □
```

```
    1  1  1  0
 −     9  1  1
 ─────────────
       1  9  9
```

(2 marks)

30(b)

```
         6 □ □
      ┌────────
    7 │ □ 4 □ 4
```

```
         6  3  2
      ┌──────────
    7 │ 4  4  2  4
        4  2
        ─────
           2  2
           2  1
           ─────
              1  4
              1  4
              ─────
                 0
```

(2 marks)

Printed in Great Britain
by Amazon